Stop Being Reasonable

Stop Being Reasonable

How We Really Change Our Minds

Eleanor Gordon-Smith

PublicAffairs

New York

Chapters 4 and 5 contain material that readers may find confronting or disturbing.

PublicAffairs

Hachette Book Group

1290 Avenue of the Americas, New York, NY 10104

www.publicaffairsbooks.com

@Public_Affairs

Printed in the United States of America

Originally published in hardcover and ebook by NewSouth in May 2019; published by Scribe UK in July 2019

First US Edition: October 2019

Published by PublicAffairs, an imprint of Perseus Books, LLC, a subsidiary of Hachette Book Group, Inc. The PublicAffairs name and logo is a trademark of the Hachette Book Group.

The publisher is not responsible for websites (or their content) that are not owned by the publisher.

Library of Congress Control Number: 2019948408

ISBNs: 978-1-5417-3044-1 (hardcover), 978-1-5417-3043-4 (ebook)

LSC-C

10 9 8 7 6 5 4 3 2 1

To Claire, Michael, Marie, Jacqui, Brush,

and their grace when I was sixteen

and always right.

Contents

Contents

introduction

Everything Was Protein Powder and Nothing Hurt

Somewhere in the technological belt of California, where the only thing more precisely engineered than the software is the people—or maybe the people's teeth—lives an organization called the Center for Applied Rationality.[1] For the low price of $3,900, the center will sell you a four-day workshop on reasoning, during which participants eat, sleep, and take part in nine hours of back-to-back activities together daily under one (presumably rationally designed) roof. This year, just like every other year, the center will receive hundreds of applications from people who want to attend because, as they put it, "Everyone I know is irrational, and I want to fix them."[2]

These folks make for an easy punch line, a good group to laugh at. But it turns out many of us make a version of the

1

same mistake when we think about persuasion. We think we know what it is to change our minds rationally, and the only question is why other people don't do it more often. The ideal mind change is calm. It reacts to reasoned argument. It responds to facts, not to our sense of self or the people around us. It resists the siren song of emotion. People like to talk about the public sphere—if there is such a thing, then its convex edge reflects this idealized image back at us. Think of the number of programs dedicated to the mind-changing magic of two sides saying opposite things: *Meet the Press*, *State of the Union*, *Face the Nation*. The branding of these things often bakes in a little reward: how brave I am, for attending the Festival of *Dangerous* Ideas; how clever, for my subscription to the *Intelligence* Squared debates. The proper way to reason, at least according to our present ideal, is to discard ego and emotion and step into a kind of disinfected argumentative operating theater where the sealed air-conditioning vents stop any everyday fluff from floating down and infecting the sterilized truth.

Years ago I used to share this view. I'll tell you why, even though it will rightly make you want to take my lunch money: when I was in school, I was a champion debater, which is another way of saying I spent my weekends wearing a blazer and telling people in precisely timed intervals exactly how wrong they were. My teammates and I constructed arguments for twenty hours a week, putting premises in the crosshairs with the unblinking accuracy of people whose whole egos were on the line. We weren't bad, either. Eventually, we made it to the world championships in Qatar, where we wore blazers embroidered with the Australian coat of arms in gold and competed in what looked, in hindsight, like a scene in an apocalypse movie just before the purge begins: all of us in matching uniforms on fleets of white buses being shepherded through the desert haze to auditoriums where we would sit locked up together for an hour surrounded by stopwatch-wielding officials. Debating left me with an attitude toward persuasion that was as precise as Euclidean geometry: find the foundation; show why it's wrong. Buttress analysis with evidence. Emotion is for decorative flourishes only—do not expect it to be load bearing. Of course, I knew you *could* change minds by appealing to things like emotion or your opponents' sense of self, but doing that seemed kind of base. It felt nobly sportsmanlike to arm yourself with argument alone. It was the intellectual equivalent of turning up at dawn for your duel with your pistols shined and paces counted: it was how you were *meant* to fight.

This perspective began to change after I produced a piece for the radio show *This American Life* in 2016. The idea had seemed simple: turn around to my own catcallers—men who had wolf-whistled or made sexual comments to me on the street—and try to reason them out of doing it again. I spent hours giving these men all the evidence, all the reasoning, all the fancy footwork with premises. But after dozens of con-versations, I walked away defeated. Over and over again, they

3

walked away from our conversations as sure as they'd ever been that it was okay to grab, yell at, or follow women on the street.

These men didn't seem fundamentally irrational or unstuck from reality—in fact, in a funny sort of way, I quite liked a few of them. One told me he modeled his courtship rituals on the animal kingdom: "I'm just another paradise bird, flaunting my shit," he said triumphantly, as though this explained everything that needed to be explained. That's a good line. He made me laugh. But I couldn't change their minds. The experience deflated me not just as a person and as a woman but as someone who had always been optimistic about our ability to talk each other into better beliefs. We finished recording in November 2016, right after the US general election, which set a grim backdrop for a newly found pessimism toward rational debate and persuasion.

But when the piece aired, a strange thing happened. I was inundated with interview requests. Could I write a ten-step guide to changing minds? Would I accept an award for the successful use of rational persuasion in public? What advice did I have for talking people out of being workplace harassers? I was astonished. Large numbers of people had apparently listened to my conversations with catcallers on the radio—conversations that I had walked away from feeling dejected and defeated—and heard instead instances of persuasive success. I think the explanation is that these conversations bore a sort of Madame Tussauds–like resemblance to what we think good mind changes look like. I said one thing, my catcallers said the opposite thing, and each of us tried to explain why we were right. I had stayed calm; they had been prepared to hear me out. I had used statistics. It looked for all the world like a rational debate, and the fact that I had failed to change any minds with this approach disappeared under the shadow of the unquestioned assumption that I deserved congratulations for even trying. I started to smell a rat—a big one that lives in the sewers and never takes a shower.

Everywhere we look we see the gospel that reasoned argument is the currency of persuasion and that the "right" way to change our minds is by entering a sort of gladiatorial contest of ideas where we leave the personal behind. But what if our eagerness to congratulate each other for employing that ideal stops us from asking whether it is worth aspiring to at all?

Another reason I started to look at persuasion differently is that I started working in academic philosophy, where it takes about two minutes to hit a wall of unanswered questions about what reason actually is or what it asks of us. You can't stay wedded to the importance of reasoned debate when you don't even know what it is to be reasonable in the first place. Maybe you think it's simple, that being reasonable just means believing things in proportion to the evidence, but if that was your first thought, then please accept my condolences as you plummet backward down the rabbit hole.

What counts as evidence? Are sensory perceptions evidence? Or feelings, like empathy? If not, what licenses your belief that other people's suffering matters? When is there enough evidence to believe something? Do different beliefs require different amounts of evidence, and, if so, what sets them? Could anything else have a bearing on what we should believe, like the costs of error? And what sort of "should" are we using when we ask, "What should we believe?" Are we aiming at truth, or at morality, or are they in some way the same goal? Are the standards for believing mathematical or scientific truths different from moral or interpersonal ones, or is there no distinction? What's the responsible way to respond to the news that someone as intelligent as you, in possession of as much evidence as you, believes a different conclusion? Should you downgrade your confidence in your own view? If so, why?

There is a bigger question underneath it all: When is it ever possible to know anything? Thousands of years before Descartes wondered what it was possible to know, Greek philosopher Sextus Empiricus had already fathered skepticism by answering, "Nothing." This is a possibility so genuinely frightening that people prefer to parse it as a silly thought experiment about whether we're in *The Matrix* than to engage with the awful specter it raises. One philosopher who took that specter seriously was Stanley Cavell, who spent years trying to answer the skeptic's challenge and whose work is so captivating to a certain sort of reader that for years, two big East Coast university libraries in the United States refused to restock his books. There was no point—students just did not bring them back. ["How do we *stop*?" Cavell wrote. "How do we learn that what we need is not more knowledge but the willingness to forgo knowing?"[3]]

Over millennia these questions about what to believe, when, and why have pinballed back and forth between the most blisteringly intelligent people of their day, and still nobody has the settled answers. Not all that long ago, on philosophy's timescale, Pittsburgh philosopher John McDowell wrote his seminal work *Mind and World*, which wonders among other things what sort of thing rationality could be. Reviewing it, Rutgers-by-way-of-MIT professor Jerry Fodor wrote that "we're very close to the edge of what we know how to talk about at all sensibly."[4]

I do not have the poetic instincts or vocabulary to be able to describe, against that backdrop, what hair-tearing frustration it is to see the concept of "rationality" bandied about in public without any acknowledgment of the longevity and complexity of these questions. Instead, pundits who take themselves to be the chief executors of rationality simply assert things about what it is to be reasonable by taking as bedrock the very things that still remain to be proved.

You will see people speak as though "being reasonable" is just being unemotional, as British member of Parliament Michael Gove did when he appeared on *Good Morning Britain* after the fire in Grenfell Tower, speaking in tones usually reserved for children who've had too much sugar. "We can put victims first [by] responding with *calmness*," he told Piers Morgan. "It doesn't help anyone, understandable though it is, to let emotion cloud reason.…And you, [Piers], have a responsibility to look *coolly* at this situation."

The idea seems to be that being emotional precludes being rational and that we can select only one way of being at a time. Antonin Scalia, the former US Supreme Court justice, argued along these lines when he wrote, "Good judges pride themselves on the rationality of their rulings and the suppression of their personal proclivities, including most especially their emotions.… [O]vert appeal to emotion is likely to be regarded as an insult. ('What does this lawyer think I am, an impressionable juror?')"[5] Where did we get this confidence that emotion has no place in reasoning? Who says emotions can't themselves be rational? Many philosophers think they can be: at minimum, it's an open question.

Or you will see people speak as though "being rational" is just the task of getting your behavior to match your goals, an inheritance from an economic model of the rational consumer. You want to save more money? Here's an app. You want to exercise more? Here's a morning routine. Geoff Sayre-McCord, an impossibly genial philosopher at the University of North Carolina at Chapel Hill who collects motorcycles and writes about belief, told a story at a Princeton workshop on the ethics of belief that illustrates how slippery this idea of "rationality" can be. An economist friend of his gives a speech at a conference, espousing the idea that "rationality" governs the space between our goals and how we act, but has nothing much to say about *which* goals we should pursue. Hours later, at the pub, the economist laments his teenage son's failure to set the "proper" goals: "All he does is play drums and drive around with his friends! He doesn't study; he doesn't think about his future. He's being *so* irrational."

Or worse, you will see people speak as though being reasonable demands waiting perpetually for more evidence, as they do during any publicized allegation of sexual assault. "Innocent until proven guilty!" we hear, as dozens of women come forward. "We have to wait for the evidence!" If testimony doesn't count as evidence, what does? Why is it that for any other criminal act, testimony and the balance of probability make it rational to believe "that guy did it," but in this case they do not?

At the same time as all of these apparent confidences about what it means to be reasonable, we also seem firmly convinced that there is one issue that rationality cannot decide: the question of what morality is and what it demands of us. I cannot count the number of times I have told a dentist or train-seat companion that I work on rationality and ethics, only to hear the confident reply, "But morality's just a matter of opinion!" That may well be true, but it also may not be: the best and brightest philosophical minds disagree over whether moral truths exist or can be reached by logic, yet everywhere I go I see it taken as obvious that moral questions fall outside the jurisdiction of reason—every time I teach Ethics 101, my students come into the class repeating the demure refrain "Everyone's entitled to their opinion."

Here's my point: in our haste to congratulate ourselves for being reasonable, we accidentally untied the very notion of rationality from its rich philosophical ancestry and from the complexity of actual human minds, and now the idea of being reasonable that underpins our public discourse has little to do with helping us find our way back to the truth, or to each other, and altogether more to do with selling us $3,900 workshops and an anesthetized dream of an optimized future where everything is protein powder and nothing hurts.

The strange thing is that most of us are already suspicious of this image of "rational debate." How many times have you seen a TV panel discussion in which the defender of one view turned to their opponent and said, "You know, actually, that's a pretty good point"? Ever? And when you have changed your mind about something close to you, was it because of a rational argument, or was the process something stranger and more difficult to map, like a subterranean rumble you weren't aware of until it was over, or a single moment in which the old facts cast a new shadow? Most of us learned long ago that changing our minds about something that matters—whether we were right to act the way we did, whether to believe what we are being told, whether we are in love—is far messier than any topiaried argument will allow. Those spaces aren't debates. They are moments between people—messy, flawed, baggage-carrying people—and our words have to navigate a space where old hurts and concealed fears and calcified beliefs hang stretched between us like spun sugar, catching the light for only a second or two before floating out of view again.

In that space, reason and logic don't work the way we're trained to think they will. Language doesn't even work. Where once stood your helpful little army of words marshaling themselves into formations that express yourself and your point, there now stands a mob of rogue mercenaries inflicting damage in ways you can't even understand, let alone apologize for. You make the right phonetic noises for something like "I'm sorry," but what appears in the common ground is closer to "You're overreacting" or "I had a really good excuse," and nothing seems further away than reason when your little "I'm sorry" looks to the other person like a weird molten Frankenstein of insult and shame. Wittgenstein said that if a lion could speak, we wouldn't understand him. Sometimes I think it's not just lions.

So why, when we know that changing our minds is as tangled and difficult and messy as we are, do we stay so wedded to the thought that rational debate is the best way to go about it? Why do we hold our ideal of rationality fixed and try to mold ourselves around it, instead of the other way around? Why do we still think the important question is a psychological one about how we *do* change our minds, instead of a philosophical one about how we *should*?

I now think that our typical views about how we should change minds are not just wrong but bad for all of us, and my hope is that this book will go some way to showing why. You are about to read a series of true stories about people who changed their minds while under the kind of pressure that gives a person the bends. Many of them tell their stories here for the first time.

Some of them are stories of revelation, like the moment when Susie discovered her husband had been telling a criminal lie since he was twelve years old and began to fear for herself and her young child, or when Peter opened his ailing mother's mail for her and discovered she wasn't who he'd thought she was, or when Dylan quit the strict apocalypse-heralding religious sect he'd been raised in after more than twenty years as a believer. Others are stories about not knowing what to believe, like the shifting cognitive sands Upper-

Class English Gentleman Alex found himself in when he finished a stint on a reality TV program that had trained him as a London bouncer, only to realize he was no longer entirely sure which of those two identities he'd been faking. Or there's the former navy pilot Nicole, who has spent years mired in confusion after alleging as a six-year-old that her mother had abused her, then reading an exposé about her own case many years later that argued the abuse may never have occurred.

Each of these people did something in their mind change that defies the public orthodoxies about how we "ought" to reason. These are not stories of neat deliberation. These people were influenced by the sorts of things our rational pundits tell us to check at the door: their sense of self, or what they'd been told, or how they felt, or the costs of uncertainty, or who (not what) they believed, or even whom they loved. These stories show us, in vivid detail, that sometimes it can be perfectly rational to change our minds on the basis of these things.

Part of why I tell these stories is because I hope they can give us a blueprint for our own most difficult persuasive projects.

When we set out to change people's views, it's easy to forget just how resistant minds are to changing. It's easy to feel, as I did when I spoke to my catcallers, like we've spent a whole lot of conversational energy ticking all the boxes in the rational persuasion manual and been rewarded with nothing but a frustrating stalemate. It is a uniquely teeth-grinding moment: not just to fail to persuade, but to have no idea what went wrong. My hope is that in telling these stories here, we can learn to better diagnose these moments and, more optimistically, to see what happens when things do click. The people in these stories pulled off massive mind changes using altogether human tools of reasoning like trust, and credibility, and their sense of self, and their emotions, and their ways of avoiding the shame of having to reckon with the fact that they were wrong. If we can understand those tools a little better, and see them as rational as well as practical, then we may be able to use them in changes of mind we most want to accomplish.

That goes for our own changes of mind, not just other people's. Though few of us will find ourselves in situations like the ones in this book, we very often find ourselves asking the questions these people had to: *Who am I really? What if I've been wrong? Who am I without this belief? What should I think?* Often it's not at all clear how we get out of these tangles. I used to very seriously believe in God, for instance. I have the physical memory of carpet pressing into my bare knees at school as I prayed for the soul of Nguyen Tuong Van, who was due to be executed in Singapore that day for drug trafficking. But just as vivid as that memory is my certainty that I didn't change my mind because of a rational argument. I just noticed one day that it had been a while since I'd believed in God. And often we could use a more definitive way out of those tangles: I also used to believe I was in love with someone who splintered furniture when I spoke to other men, and I'd have given two of my toes and probably an eyeball for the syllogism that could have changed my mind about that. But it doesn't exist. Uprooting these foundational beliefs and working out what to do with the clods of selfhood they shook off on the way out was just too messy a job for a tidy argument. If we can find an ideal of rationality that doesn't berate us for that messiness, we may find it easier to change our own minds when it matters most.

And partly I tell these stories because if our ideal of rational persuasion turns out to be wrong, we had better stop constructing our public discourse around it, and soon. We broadcast opinions grosser than the stuff they scrape out of clogged sewage pipes because we are so confident that rational debate can work, and we do this despite fairly good evidence that just entertaining a thought makes people more likely to believe it. Producers, newspapers, and event managers give airtime to racist, sexist, science-denying speakers by saying we need to Challenge These People, but seldom do those same producers and event managers seem to have researched how to make those challenges successful or sought advice from professionals who have spent years embedded with these ideologies studying how, if ever, they change. We risk all the harms that come from giving these people a platform simply because we're so confident that we're the ones who know how persuasion should work. *Everyone I know is irrational, and I want to fix them.*

It strikes me as a colossal tragedy that in deference to our rusted-out idea of persuasion, we structured our public discourse around regimented debates, leaving persuasive strategies built on how we *actually* think to the used-car salespeople of the cognitive landscape: advertising executives, or lawyers, or actual used-car salespeople, whose highest aspiration for their insights is that they might better pry purchases or decisions out of the unsuspecting public. It is as though beginning in the muddy reality of being a person was a fitting strategy for professions that never hoped to leave that muddy reality, but for professions whose highest aspiration was truth, enlightenment, reason, or progress, the chaos of actual life was not just useless but distracting. There was too much emotion in the ordinary, too much talking, too many other people, none of which makes a good basis for changing your mind—or so we're told.

And so the people who trusted this model of rational discourse were advised to retreat from the messy and the real, declaring progressively more and more ways of connecting to the world or other people to have no place in a proper argument. Or they spent their time reading manuals about how to spot a fallacy and dutifully tuning into each new broadcast debate trying not to wonder why it felt so hollow. And now those of us who felt like we should have been the most useful warriors for persuasion sit suspended, alone, on syllogistic crags far above a world where Nazis are back, and so is polio, it's prohibitively expensive to fight either, and the oceans are rising while we tell each other to just "be reasonable."

Is it just me, or do we need to get a lot better at changing minds—very fucking quickly?

chapter one

A Treatise on the Ways Your Dick Is Not Like This Burrito

In the union of the sexes...it is necessary that one should have the power and the will, and the other should make little resistance. Once this principle is established it follows that woman is expressly formed to please the man.

—JEAN-JACQUES ROUSSEAU

As for Rousseau's remarks...that [women] have naturally, that is from their birth, independent of education, a fondness for dolls, dressing, and talking, they are so puerile as not to merit a serious refutation.

—MARY WOLLSTONECRAFT

Scene: A Mexican-food establishment in Kings Cross, Sydney's nightclub district. Approximately seven in the evening. Cast of characters: me, exhibiting what Germans call *weltschmerz*, or "world-weariness"; Mark, a nearby man; another man sitting with Mark whose name I have forgotten and to whom I will therefore refer as "Mark 2." A microphone is on the table in front of me, as I'm taking a break from recording. A burrito—a big, proper, carby, cheesy burrito thick as my arm and wrapped in foil—the high point of my night.

Brief pause, bite, ill-timed eye contact.

"I'd let you wrap your mouth 'round my burrito," says one of the Marks.

I had been recording conversations with my catcallers for the radio program *This American Life*.[1] Men who catcalled women on the street had confused me since I was a kid and the first man slowed his car at the corner to shout something at me that Doppler-shifted away before it could be understood. Since then, the assortment of things I've seen men say and do on streets seems to map out such a bizarre constellation of graphic sexism and boyish hope that I have never been able to understand it. Is there a single motivational thread connecting whistles to shouted compliments and compliments to unwelcome grabbings? For weeks I tried to find out. I'd take a microphone and a recorder out at night and walk the nightlife district in Sydney's Kings Cross, where the sky is lit by neon and the gutters paved with vomit. I'd wait for the inevitable catcalls and then turn around and ask, "What were you hoping for just then?"

Most of the men stuck around to give an answer. There was Sebastian, a strip-club carnival barker whose job was to shepherd passing groups of young men into a nearby gentlemen's club, where they'd sit eagerly in big-spending rows, bursting out of their too tight shirts like sausages splitting their skin. When I passed Sebastian for the first time, he made a gesture in the air like he was fondling a pair of invisible ghost breasts, and when I asked him if he thought women enjoyed that sort of thing, he said he'd met his girlfriend by catcalling her. I asked if I could use his phone to ring her and check this. I could not.

There was Duncan, a Scottish backpacker waiting for his friend to come out of a nearby liquor store, who whistled at me as I walked past. He was keen for me to know that he had a master's degree—"Never judge a book by its cover!"—and told me that sometimes when he whistled, girls said, "Oh, thank you, baby." There was the unbelievably high kid whose name is nearly inaudible on the recording because his jaw was busy swinging through the Hunter S. Thompsonesque quantity of drugs he had definitely not consumed and who nearly cried when he told me he just didn't know how to talk to women.

And there were the Marks, one of whom said the thing about the burrito, and who almost immediately started commiserating with me about men. "You think *we're* bad," one of them said as we stood clustered outside the burrito place, "then you should meet our boss. He looks like Humpty Dumpty, but he thinks he's God's gift to women. The other day I was with a girl, and he came up and grabbed her hips and said, 'Hey, baby, let's get a coffee.' She started laughing, but she asked him not to touch [her] again. And he got the point, but...actually he doesn't get the point. He's really stubborn."

I was surprised that these men agreed to be interviewed. I happen to own an especially mean-looking recorder, the sort with an unforgiving red "record" light that stares at you un- blinkingly while you speak, so you can never quite forget its presence or its ruthless on-record-ification. It looks like the sort of thing tabloid journalists would chase you with if you were a corrupt mayor emerging from a nasty court appearance, so I was braced for the possibility that it would make these po- tential interviewees scatter like the rats in *Ratatouille* when the old woman first discovers them in her roof. In fact, that happened only once—a guy yelled "Feminist!" and pushed his friends away from me. But more often, these men gave me a surprising amount of their souls in exchange for the chance to be on air. "I love this!" one told me. "I love being interviewed!"

I was surprised, too, by how not insane they seemed. I had met these men because of their lewd or loud impositions, but once we started speaking they were often funny, gentle, and easy to talk to. Like Sebastian, the strip-club guy, who grew strangely fatherly as the nights wore on: One night I interviewed four very drunk men who took issue with the project and stood around me in a horseshoe, glaring, while I had my back to a wall, and Sebastian wandered over just close enough for his presence to be felt. Another night he saw me looking worn down and said, "You're doing good work, darling." I'd expected more of these men to react like the glarers: ready to erupt, as though I had trespassed just by speaking. Instead, the overwhelming majority did not seem unreachable, irrational, or as though they were speaking a fundamentally different language from mine. I was quietly optimistic about my chances of changing their minds with the power of a Rational Conversation.

But when I asked them why they catcalled women, they gave an inconsistent recitation of motivations, each one sitting uneasily with the one before it:

"A guy just does it for attention."

"I'm looking for a reaction, any reaction."

"I'm looking to meet someone! Start a conversation, try to see if she's into it."

"To be honest with you, I don't really think a guy has 'motivation.' I think it's just pack mentality."

Over several weeks I had dozens of conversations with catcallers, and almost every one began with this strange mash of motivations. It was frustrating: you can't begin to change a person's mind if you can't even work out what he thinks.

Eventually, thanks to the editorial skill of Neil Drumming and Ira Glass at *This American Life*, I learned to ask a different question: "Does it matter to you if she enjoys it?" Duncan-of-the-master's-degree nodded vigorously. His friend emerged from the liquor store in time to ask what we were chatting about and added, "Oh, yeah, I don't think Duncan's hustling at women in a disrespectful way."

A different night, I met the best man out at a bachelor party, and when I asked him the same question, he said, "A hundred percent! It's like teasing—they love it." He told me he'd ordered high-visibility vests and hard hats for the party so his friends could "dress up like misogynistic arseholes for the night," but his friends had announced, "We're not wearing that shit." (It's worth mentioning that many construction companies around the world have immediate and severe penalties for workers who engage in street harassment, but stereotypes die slow.) Despite not "dressing up" as a misogynist, the groom-to-be still hobbled over wearing an inflatable ball and chain on his ankle to ask if I'd come out with them. He did a helpful mime of a blow job on the microphone so I got the point.

"See, it's funny!" said his best man, doubled over laughing.

When I asked Sebastian the same question, he was emphatic: "It's nice! It's nice when a man says hello!" He deployed a kind of "Certified Nonsexist" badge to prove he wouldn't do it if he didn't think women liked it. "If I see anyone around here hitting a girl or anything like that, I stop him," he said. "I protect women. I'm a gentleman."

The Ways Your Dick Is Not Like This Burrito

In my regimented brain, the strategy was simple: find out what made these men believe that women enjoy being cat-called, and replace it with my saying, "We don't."

First: What evidence *did* they have? Most of them cited the reaction they got from the women they spoke to or touched or whistled at. Actually, Sebastian just said that women *"have* to love it!"—as though it was a determined metaphysical truth revealed by the laws of nature—but most of them went with the reaction thing.

Nowhere was the belief "smiling is evidence" more strongly held than in the minds of two friends named Zac and Mike, whom I met walking past a burrito place—no, not the same one, and yes, I ate a lot of burritos while working on this story. As the pair of them crossed the alley diagonally in front of me, Zac shouted something about lips and kisses. When I went over to talk to him, he noticed the fluffy windshield I had on my microphone to stop some of the *whoop-whoop-whoop* wind noise you get recording in narrow alleys between tall buildings. "This wouldn't by any chance be symbolizing anything about you, would it?" he grinned. "Not saying there's anything wrong with that! I'm down for a ticklish encounter, but I would prefer skin to skin. If you were asking."

"All right—come here, come here," I said. "We just met. And you just yelled something out at me. And I'm walking around trying to find out why guys do that. So what was it? What were you hoping for?"

Mike spoke first. "To catch the lady's attention! I could have just walked past you and thought, 'Oh, there she goes. She looks gorgeous, but I'm never gonna see her again.' But you throw a chance out there in the water, and you might get a bite."

Zac did a little fishing-rod pantomime and an alarmingly good impression of the reel-'em-in noise. He agreed with Mike. They had a sort of double-act rhythm worked out where a single thought or joke would volley between them so that you had to look at Zac and then Mike and then Zac again to get its whole delivery, as though you were watching a tennis match.

"Just you coming and talking to us right now, that's a win!" Zac said. "You're not looking away, walking the other way—you're engaged with my presence, with my mate, and it's all come from me shouting shit at you! I want her to get enjoyment out of what I yell at her. In no way do I want her to feel insecure or uncomfortable. I'm never gonna say anything rude or abusive. I'm yelling complimenting shit—I want the girl to think she's important for the night. Even though it might just be two seconds, at least someone's acknowledging that she looks good."

"So you think that girls like it?" I asked, trying to be as explicit as possible about the thing I knew I'd need to disprove.

"One hundred percent," Zac agreed.

"What percentage of the time do girls come over, or say they really liked it?" I asked.

"I'd say you're the 1 percent, so I'd say about 99 percent don't," Zac admitted.

"So [then] why do you think girls like it?"

"Because of the smirk, and the smile on the face...I've done ruder things, like I've gone along to groups of girls on the street and smacked one of their arses. I slap the arse of one girl, and all the rest are fixated on, like, 'Oh my god, why was *her* arse slapped?' And she, in front of all her friends, she feels like, 'Oh my god, *my* arse was slapped by a complete random!' It's the singling out. It doesn't actually matter if it's the hottest arse in the group..."

"What did the last girl you did that to do?"

"She pulled her thigh and butt cheek away, like 'Ahhh!' and then all her friends were like—"

Mike demonstrated what all her friends had been like with an impression of a girlish giggle-laugh.

"Exactly!" said Zac, gesturing at the space Mike had giggled into with a magician-like sweep of his open palm. "I'm not doing anything wrong," he concluded. "I'm complimenting a girl's arse in public."

"You think that smacking a girl's arse in public isn't doing anything wrong?" I said, almost laughing too.

"No. I judge it, I judge the situation, whether an arse slap would be...complimenting or not."

"Okay. And am I the first person who's ever come over to you?"

"Yes! You are!" Zac said. "You're the first that's actually come over and gone, 'Hey, I have appreciated your comment.'"

Mike stifled a laugh with his fist. "She didn't even say that."

"Oh yeah." Zac turned to him, laughing back.

Zac and Mike told me more stories about how girls reacted, every story accompanied by an impression of a sort of prom-night shriek that sounded exactly like Fran Drescher's character in *The Nanny*.

"Oy, you know what he does?" Mike said, nodding in Zac's direction. "We'll be out, and if there's a group of girls, he'll go up to them, right, and he'll say, 'My mate thinks I can't pick you up.' And then he picks them up! And throws them over his shoulder and spins them around. And they're always like—"

He made a drawn-out *eeeee* sound, like the noise a rapidly deflating balloon would make if it saw a cute puppy, and flapped his hands around in that drying-my-freshly-painted-nails-type motion. "They love it!" he said triumphantly.

As evidence goes, this should have been easy enough to discredit. You know and I know that there is a fair amount of inferential space between "I see women smiling" and "I'm sure they're enjoying themselves" because women often smile and laugh out of nervousness, or fear, or even just as a way to get out of a social situation with as little friction as possible. I said this to Zac and Mike: that the smiles and laughs might in fact be evidence that women are uncomfortable.

"I actually kind of feel a little bit bad now," said Zac. "Not heaps, but a little bit. That's a sad thing that exists in our society, isn't it, that an arse slap cannot just be taken as a compliment. Which isn't the way that it should be, but I can understand that it happens. But I'm not going to say that I'm going to stop slapping arses."

"Why aren't you going to stop doing it?"

"Because when I do it, it's in the friendliest way possible. I'm all smiles, they're all smiles, and it's kind of like this celebration that we all share. I'm having a mad night, they didn't know that they were having a mad night, but now"—he windmilled his hand down in a slapping motion—"*tunk*! They are."

"But that's what I'm saying to you…You have no way of knowing whether the smiles and the laughs are genuine, or whether they're—"

"Aw, boohoo," interjected Mike. "He didn't slap your arse and then grab your wrist and try to take you around the corner—he slapped your arse and then [it's done]. It's like you step out on a curb, and you see a car, and you go, 'Oh shit, I'm scared' but then you step back and it's all fine again."

"But if you're the reason that someone has that moment of feeling scared, why do you think that's an okay thing to make people feel?"

"But what should we *do*, honey?" Mike said, sounding genuinely confused.

"People can't base their lives on this small-percentage shit!" said Zac. "The majority of people want to do what we're doing—have fun, slap arses, say things across the road—and it goes no further."

I tried again. It isn't about what they're *trying* to do, I suggest; it's about how they come across.

"But you can't speak for all girls!" Mike protested.

"This is all subjective," Zac added. "I'm sorry that what I said may have brought around those feelings, but it's individual. It's an *opinionated* view of men screaming at them. Okay, you don't like it—I'm not saying everyone likes it—but I've seen the reaction in a lot of girls, and it's a short moment of, like, 'Ha ha!' It's just a boost of confidence."

"Every girl has a different level of sensitivity, and I'm feeling from you that your sensitivity is *way* high," Mike said to me. "Every girl's different, so we might have said something that offended you. Let's move on."

I got the same reaction from other men when I told them that the smiles and laughs they saw might not be proof that women enjoy it.

"Nah, nah, I'm not frightening anyone. With a face like this? Naaahhh," said Sebastian.

"No, no, they love it," said the bucks-night best man. "You have to see it."

I have to see it? I've *done* it. I feign amusement or attraction or wide-eyed admiration all the time in the company of men I don't trust. An unseen something sits down at my cognitive controls and drives my voice up two octaves and winches my smile an inch too wide. But somehow these men didn't seem to register that I was a woman and that I therefore had better knowledge than they did about the sort of person we were trading hypotheses about. Instead, they disagreed with me as though they were speaking from a comparably good vantage point, like we were all scientists peering down at these mute female creatures. When Simone de Beauvoir wrote her seminal work *The Second Sex*, she spent considerable time dissecting the myth that women are mysterious and hard to read (which came as a surprise to her publisher, who had picked up her work expecting a zoological treatise on sex). The feminine mystery "permits an easy explanation of all that appears inexplicable," she wrote. "[The] man who 'does not understand' a woman is happy to substitute an objective resistance for a subjective deficiency of mind."[2] I like to think de Beauvoir would have laughed at these conversations, the photonegative of the phenomenon she had in mind. These men saw no possibility that there could be something they did not understand:

But the girls laugh.

Those laughs are designed to mislead you.

No, trust me. They're not.

It was as though everybody in *The Truman Show* had finally revealed to Truman that his whole world was a TV production set, and instead of taking this as new information he calmly told the set designer they were wrong. *What?* thinks the set designer. *I helped design it. How can you know better than I do whether it's real or not?*

I should have tried yelling, "I AM A WOMAN," but if I'd done that they would have just told me what they told me anyway, over and over again: "You can't speak for all girls." And besides, then I'd have been in trouble for yelling.

I spoke to Zac and Mike for close to an hour that night. For nearly half that time, we stayed stuck on the question of whether girls liked being catcalled.

"But you can't speak for all girls! You can't—it's not…," Mike said, over and over, as confused by our impasse as I was. Then they had to go; they had a gig to get to.

"You have made me more aware of the ways girls think," said Zac, "and I completely understand that. But it's not gonna make me change anything."

We exchanged numbers in the alleyway, and as Zac typed mine in he sang, almost to himself, "Elea-nor, Elea-nor, do not ignore, Elea-nor."

"Is there *anything* I could say to make you change your mind about yelling this stuff at girls?" I tried, before I let them go.

"You could say you'll spend the night with us," said Mike.

There is widespread confidence that the best way to defeat noxious arguments is to face them head-on and prove them false, ideally in front of an audience. That confidence was there in seventeenth-century England when Parliament's licensing restrictions meant only certain works could be printed and John Milton, author of *Paradise Lost*, argued against those restrictions in part by saying that defenders of truth should welcome the chance to hear and refute rival views: "Who ever knew Truth put to the worse, in a free and open encounter?"[3] That confidence was there when John Stuart Mill wrote two centuries later in his treatise *On Liberty* (1859) that interpersonal argument was a crucial part of our progress toward truth: "[Man] is capable of rectifying his mistakes, by discussion and experience. Not by experience alone. There must be discussion.... Wrong opinions and practices gradually yield to fact and argument; but facts and arguments, to produce any effect on the mind, must be brought before it. Very few facts are able to tell their own story, without comments to bring out their meaning."

These are the founders of the free-speech tradition from whom we inherit many of our ideas about discourse and debate, so it's little wonder that the same confidence in discussion was there in 2017 when the *New York Times* responded to reader criticism of its profile of a white nationalist by saying, "What we think is indisputable...is the need to shed more light, not less, on the most extreme corners of American life and the people who inhabit them,"[4] or when Marine Le Pen, leader of France's far-right front, gave a heavily protested speech at the Oxford Union, and students responded to protesters by saying, "We need to listen to her....We should engage with her on a rational level and ask her some intelligent questions." That confidence was also there in 2009 when the BBC's *Question Time* booked an appearance by Nick Griffin, then leader of the far-right British National Party, and the prime minister at the time, Gordon Brown, said, "It will be a good opportunity to expose what [the BNP] are about.... [A]nybody who listens to what they are really about will find that what they are saying is unacceptable," and it was there in 2014 when the cofounder of Sydney's Festival of Dangerous Ideas scheduled Uthman Badar's talk "Honour Killings Are Morally Justified" and responded to protests by arguing that "dangerous ideas are best exposed to the light of reason and discernment." The festival, the cofounder said, aimed to allow people to "calibrate their own thoughts about the issues that they encounter, knowing better the character of the dangerous idea that they hope to defeat."[5] The thread of philosophical thought is clear: the rigorous clash of argument will bring us closer to the truth.

But the promise that debates defeat falsehoods starts to fall apart when we learn that words do not work the same way for everyone. What use is all that legislative protection of your right to speak if, when you do speak, you're not even heard? Words are not just vessels for ideas to enter the coliseum of argument. Words are attached to people, and some people arrive in debates preflattened by their opponents' expectations such that they are mistrusted before they have even spoken or assumed unintelligent before they have made their case. What chance does rational debate have to defeat falsehoods if it is possible for the people with the right idea to mount their argument perfectly well but then, as they turn to see their words appear on the Debate Scoreboard, find that their words have simply disappeared?

The truth is that if our policy makers and public intellectuals paid half as much attention to contemporary philosophy as they do to the philosophy of three-hundred-year-old Bewigged Gentlemen, they would know that this phenomenon isn't just possible but common and that it is wood rot to the foundations of rational debate.

Philosophy professor Miranda Fricker noticed this phenomenon in a recent work on what she calls "testimonial injustice," which is a professorial way of saying "the bullshit when people dismiss your words for no good reason." Fricker is a British philosopher who spent years working in ethics, feminist philosophy, and the study of knowledge, before combining them all into her foundational work "renegotiating the border" between these usually separate subdisciplines. She does this by asking how we get knowledge from each other and what injustices might live in the cases where we don't. Fricker argues that people suffer an injustice when other people's prejudices mean they "[receive] deflated credibility," as when defendants of color are dismissed by police because of their race, or when women's reports about how much pain they are in are dismissed because of their gender, or when a speaker with an accent is taken less seriously because of what their accent implies about their regional background, class, and education. These prejudices, Fricker argues, "will tend surreptitiously to inflate or deflate the credibility afforded the speaker, and sometimes this will be sufficient to cross the threshold for belief."[6]

We know these patterns from life and from fiction as well: Fricker looks at the trial at the end of Harper Lee's novel *To Kill a Mockingbird* through the lens of testimonial injustice: white woman Mayella Ewell has falsely accused African American man Tom Robinson of rape. To put it mildly, it was not the strength of Ewell's story that persuaded the jury. It was the way Robinson's words arrived in that courtroom preflattened and discredited by his race before he had even spoken. In his work on resisting these sorts of injustices, philosopher José Medina develops the point, arguing that the problem is explained by not just Tom Robinson's lack of credibility but also Mayella Ewell's surfeit: such credibility differentials were "already in place even before the defendant and his accuser walked into the witness stand.... In fact, I would say that in the trial proceedings of *To Kill a Mockingbird*, there was an entire hierarchy of credibility presumptions at play."[7] Medina, by the way, is a tenured professor at Northwestern University and formerly International Chair of Excellence in the Humanities at Carlos III University, Madrid, but before he was quite so recognizable on the Northwestern campus, students arriving early in his lecture rooms would sometimes see him and mistake him for a janitor. *An entire hierarchy of credibility presumptions was already at play.*

The Ways Your Dick Is Not Like This Burrito

It should not be surprising that the ways we allocate credibility often disadvantage the same people we always disadvantage—people who are too dark, or too feminine, or who don't seem like they're from around here. It *isn't* surprising, not if you're used to having your word dismissed by strangers, doctors, law enforcement officers, or any of the other people you have to answer to. But somehow it manages to surprise our ideal of rational debate that some words, like some speakers, are created less powerful than others. Speakers who aren't considered sufficiently credible can enter a debate and advance a point but find the other party reacts as though they had not spoken at all:

I have good evidence that women like it.

There's reason to doubt that evidence.

No, I have evidence that women like it.

Or, stranger than just disappearing, words can warp. One of the consequences of thinking your interlocutor isn't able to give you information is that you have to bend yourself in cognitive loops to find a different story about what they're trying to do with their words. Instead of thinking that they're making a point, you reach for explanations that seem more plausible to you and react to that thing instead. The problem when that happens isn't that the words go missing, but that they get bent into something totally unrecognizable to the person who spoke them, and then that twisted new creation goes on the Debate Scoreboard instead of what they meant to say. One night, in a fluorescent-lit doorway outside a hostel ominously advertising "real beds," I met Brian, who didn't technically catcall me but asked what I was up to when he saw me recording some other guys. He told me he yelled out at women now and then, and I did the usual spiel. He protested: "I'm not like that!"

I tried again. "I'm sure you're a good guy, but we can't tell from the outside who's a good guy and who we should be scared of."

He frowned kind of paternally and said, "Not being very nice now, are you?" as though the only way to parse what I was saying was as a personal accusation.

It took me a long time to see this pattern, but I think a similar thing happened when Mike told me my level of sensitivity was "way high." I said women sometimes smile out of fear, but since he genuinely did not think I was in a position to know that, he had to come up with a different explanation for what I was trying to do by speaking, and against a host of background commitments about what women are likely to do, his brain threw up the answer: "Being emotional!" If I wasn't reporting what I *knew*, I must be reporting how I *felt*.

But I hadn't said I was sensitive. I hadn't said I was insecure. I'm conscious that because I'm retelling this on the page, Mike's remark might have made you think that I was talking to these boys tremulously, through mascara-streaked tears, reciting My Feelings on Violence Against Women. I'm conscious that even here, in my own damn book, Mike's account of how emotional I was might be more believable than mine. So it might help to know that the reason I didn't say I was emotional was that I genuinely wasn't. Catcalling can be a bummer, but in the scheme of the universe I find it hard to feel much more than an internal eye roll about it, a sort of bemused flatlining. I even felt like it was prudish and a little unkind of me not to laugh when Zac made his pubic hair joke about the fluffy windshield on my microphone. I wasn't emotional—I was glad for the recording.

And it might help to know that during the entirety of my conversation with Mike and Zac, I did that autopilot too wide smile I talked about earlier. I didn't mean to. I only found out that I had afterward when I listened back to myself and heard my own jovial smile, and heard how many of Zac's jokes I laughed at, and heard the thing I didn't tell you about earlier: that when Mike told me that Zac picked girls up, literally, Mike demonstrated by picking me up and throwing me over his shoulder, and I laughed, sotto voce, in exactly the way you'd expect of someone who flaps their hands a lot like they just got their nails painted. I hate listening to it. *That* was the person whose level of sensitivity was way high: someone who laughed when they were alone with two men in an alleyway and one threw her over his shoulder. My words had warped in the common ground between us until Mike could understand them, as the worked-up reactions of a probably traumatized outlier.

I had felt an unusually sour frustration after my conversation with Zac and Mike.

Neil Drumming, producer at *This American Life*, suggested texting Zac to ask if he'd meet me again—during the day this time, and without Mike. Zac said he would, and we met on a weekday evening when both of us looked markedly different. Before I set out to meet Zac, Neil suggested I take backup: empirical research to verify what I was saying. I found surveys of women's attitudes to things like catcalling or being touched on the street and loaded them up as screenshots on my phone as I parked and walked over to where I knew Zac would be waiting.

"Let's talk about it, then," I said, after some of the strangest small talk I've ever made. "It's not just me who doesn't think it's fun—the girls that I spoke to out here say they find it creepy. [Even] you told me that you've never had a woman turn around and be like, 'That was great. Give me your number.' I have some stats, too. Sixty-seven percent of women think that an interaction in the street is going to escalate."

"Wait—67 percent believe that it's not gonna escalate?"

"No, 67 percent believe that it *will* escalate."

"To, like, something bad? Fuck, that's fucked. That's really bad."

"Eighty-five percent feel angry; 70 percent feel nervous. It's not just me. Most of us hate it."

"Well, far out. I've never heard any stats. I've kind of just gone off face value. If you're asking me if I feel bad...yeah, I feel bad if I've made anyone feel anything other than complimented. I just kind of embrace the opportunity that is arising. But maybe it's not arising and that's where I've gone wrong."

Even now when I listen to this conversation, Zac sounds so genuinely sad that I almost can't stand it. He wasn't chasing punch lines like he had been in that alley. But as quickly as it appeared, the moment dissolved back into "You can't speak for all girls."

"I'm imagining, like—a girl who's gone out on the weekend," he said, back to his regular patter pace. "[She] works in the nail salon—nothing but female contact all day. She's been looking forward to the weekend, and a guy is saying that she's good-looking! She might feel like her hair can finally come down, because she's been appreciated by someone she doesn't even know. Some girls might actually even yearn for it, go out on the streets, just walk around—I don't actually know of any stories like this actually happening—but they might go around somewhere here like the Cross and not even go into any clubs; they just want to walk around and get complimented. I'm *sure* that happens."

"Why are you sure it happens?" I asked, at this point just genuinely confused.

"Because I know dudes would be like that."

There was a long pause.

"We don't do that."

"But you can't speak for all girls! You can't speak for all girls."

"What I'm trying to say to you is: trust me, and my report of what it feels like, and women, and women's reports of what it feels like, rather than your imagining of what you *think* it might feel like. I'm giving you the evidence that it doesn't feel like that."

"It is—it's a very obnoxious thing to do, to just yell out, but that's just the way that dudes are, unfortunately."

"Is it the way that you are?"

"No, no."

After another hour of conversation, I got him to agree that he would stop slapping arses. We shook hands on it. "But compliments, I think I'm still gonna do," he said.

I'm still not totally sure whether he said it just so I'd leave him alone. I'd taken up a lot of his time. If you want to work out whether he meant it, you can hear his arse-slapping promise and almost all of that second conversation online at the *This American Life* website.

When I headed out to speak to Zac the second time, I knew I needed to stop my words from disappearing. I hadn't realized what I know now: that the whole problem when your words go missing is that it's very difficult to argue them back to life. What can you use to do that? More words?

At the time, this was all just very confusing. I'd tried to say something about the limits of the evidence, but all my interlocutors had seemed to hear was a kind of weepy charge that they, personally, were rapists. My brain was too scrambled from cascading loss of faith in our model of rational persuasion and too many late nights spent pacing Kings Cross to diagnose what had happened. But months after *This American Life* aired the complete piece—featuring my conversations with Zac alone, Zac and Mike together, and a handful of the other men—I found myself standing in a bookstore near my home in Princeton leafing through a copy of Kate Manne's book on misogyny, aptly titled *Down Girl*, when I was surprised to see my own name in a footnote. Manne, a commentator and philosophy professor at Cornell, wrote that those interviews with catcallers were evidence of "the phenomenon of men's rewriting women's minds, notwithstanding their explicit stated feelings and preferences."[8] Reading that, I felt like I finally understood what had happened. Words do not work in the same way for everyone. And when words are the currency of rational debate, rational debate does not work the same way for everyone, either.

Just understanding that rational debate is not a standardized currency had value for me. When you don't know about things like "testimonial injustice" or the ways your words can be hammered into the wrong shapes by other people's misunderstandings, hitting a persuasive stalemate can force you to choose between two unpleasant conclusions: I'm not presenting as good a case as I think I am, or my opponents are so unreasonable that talking to them could never have worked. When your opponents look, as mine did, like they're otherwise fairly reasonable, the first conclusion starts to bite. It bites even harder if your opponents are people you know or love—people we don't want to cast into the wastelands of being "unreachable."

And so we can wind up in a stalemate many of us know too well: rehearsing the same points over and over, eroding none of our opponent's certainty and quite a lot of our own sense for what could possibly be going on. It gets confusing, fast. It gets personal, fast. Am I too emotional? Why can't they hear what I keep saying? It makes you feel choked and frustrated and like language won't work, and it's no wonder that so many people terminate arguments like this by simply storming away: the one communicative gesture that can never be misunderstood.

It helps to bear these moments when we can properly see the malfunction. It isn't a failure of argument—instead it's wheel-spinning over much trickier terrain about being believed. When your starting position is being disbelieved, it's difficult to mount an argument that will get others to believe you. After all, why would they believe it? The problem here isn't that you've failed to provide good-enough evidence. The problem is that something about you prevents you from being seen as a valuable source.

We may yet find the solutions for this dynamic—it may be that there are ways to make people experience their own ignorance or that the trick is to leverage people's existing allocations of credibility, as the White Ribbon Campaign does by asking men to speak to men about gendered violence. For now, it at least helped me to quell that sense of boiling confusion to realize why one side of an argument can feel like it was perfectly rational and the other can feel like they spent the entire time banging their head on the inside of a fishbowl shouting, "Why can't anybody hear me?"

I think understanding this helps diagnose some of the problems in our public discourse, too.

Look at the way the act of "rational debate" seems a lot less fun for some people than it does for others. If some people's words routinely go missing, or get bent into shapes that better match certain stereotypes, then you might predict that those people would find less joy in recreational sword-clashing than people for whom words work the way they're meant to. Sure enough, our current climate seems to have birthed a strange sort of creature who finds the act of "rational debate" fun for its own sake. Take Rush Limbaugh, who has amassed a net worth considerably more than Beyoncé's by spending forty years at the helm of a radio program that serves decibels and far-right views by the dozen, who once said on air that women who wanted health insurance for contraception should make their sex tapes available to the public in return. Limbaugh told *Today* that most of what he did was "to satisfy the audience so they come back the next day.... I know how to yank [the media's] chain. I know how to make them spend the next two days talking about me."[9]

Or take Alex Jones, the beet-red face of views like "Sandy Hook was a government hoax" and "Robert Mueller runs a pedophile ring." When challenged, Jones says he is protected by the First Amendment and the need for rational debate, but when he was challenged for custody of his child his lawyer argued Jones was a "performance artist" who was "playing a character."

It feels like an ad hominem argument to point out that this debate-as-entertainment sort of person tends to be white and male, but perhaps I shouldn't let that stop me, since they don't seem to think it's comparably underhanded to describe women as "women," or Muslims as "Muslims," and so on. It can't be that describing people by race and gender is just a neutral description of the facts until the label reads "white man," at which point it's rude and irrelevant. In any event, we live now in an era of stunt-pilotry "rational debate" as a hobby for people whose words have never betrayed them, people who do not intimately know the frustration of their words being misheard, mistrusted, or altered by their audiences. When words reliably do what you want them to, why wouldn't you take them for a spin? The very act of debate, like the act of speaking, is more fun for some people than for others.

And rational debate isn't the only casualty of the discovery that words do not work the same way for everyone. At the serious end of the spectrum, losing control over your words means losing control over what you can do, because words are not just ways of imparting the truth; they are ways of exercising our authority as people. It was 1955 when British philosopher J. L. Austin delivered his lectures *How to Do Things with Words* to audiences at Harvard and observed that language does far more than simply describe the world: it also allows us to do things like make promises, get married, give orders, and so on.

It was even later still when Rae Langton, now a Cambridge University philosophy professor, noted that *not* being able to use words the way everyone else can amounts to not being able to perform the same actions that everyone else can. I vividly remember the first time I encountered that point in Langton's paper "Speech Acts and Unspeakable Acts."[10] It was as though someone had struck a bell in my head: governments can subjugate people, Langton explained, simply by making sure certain people's words do not function in the same way as other people's. A black South African living under apartheid could have done all the right things for the speech act of voting, but the government's rule would have disabled that power simply by legislating such that those words, from those people, did not "count" as votes. Before same-sex marriage was legal, same-sex couples were bound by legislation that meant that their words did not work in the way that everyone else's did. They could stand at an altar like anyone else, hold hands, and say "I do," but those words would not have been a marriage because the rules said that those words, from those people, did not "count." And if women's words do not always work the way they are supposed to, then neither does our capacity to authorize or prohibit how other people may treat us. Langton's imagined case of sexual assault is as horrifying as it is plausible: "Someone...might not even recognize an attempted refusal. 'Coming from her, I took it as consent,' he might say....[The woman] means what she says. She intends to refuse. She tries to refuse. But what she says misfires. Something about her, something about the role she occupies, prevents her from voicing refusal. Refusal—in that context—has become unspeakable for her."

If you doubt that this is possible, consider the much-publicized case of Luke Lazarus, the Sydney man who met eighteen-year-old Saxon Mullins in the club his father part-owned and took her outside to the alleyway that happens to be not far from where I stood speaking to Zac and Mike. When Lazarus later went on trial for rape, there was strikingly little disagreement between him and Mullins about the facts. They agree that they kissed on the dance floor. They agree that they held hands and walked away from the dance floor and that after he opened a door to the outside alley, she said she needed to go back to her friends. They agree that he told her to put her hands on the fence. They agree that he removed her underwear and that she did not physically stop him. They agree that he did not ask whether she wanted to have sex, that he told her to get on her hands and knees. They agree that she did not say "yes" and that he had anal sex with her. What they disagree about is whether he knew he was acting against her will.

Lazarus was initially found guilty of rape, but he appealed and a mistrial was called. At retrial he was found not guilty: the judge found that Mullins "in her own mind was not consenting," but that Lazarus had "reasonable grounds" for a "genuine belief" that she was.[11] A further appeal found the judge should have considered what steps Lazarus actually took to ascertain consent but that it wasn't worth a third trial.

Of course, one hypothesis is that Lazarus could not possibly have believed Mullins was consenting, in which case Sydney broadcaster Ben Fordham was right to say this to Lazarus during a 2GB radio interview: "My impression of you, from a distance, is that you are a rich kid, you're spoilt, you're powerful, you're someone who took advantage of a young eighteen-year-old girl who was drunk, who was a virgin, who didn't want to lose her virginity by having anal sex with a stranger in an alleyway....[Y]ou pushed this on her, you knew you were doing the wrong thing."[12]

But another hypothesis is in my view no less frightening: that Lazarus is sincere. That he looked at a woman who had kissed him earlier, who then fell silent and said she needed to go back to her friends, who told him she was a virgin and said nothing while he had sex with her, and that he was able to see someone who was "as happy to be there as he was." That her words and actions arrived to him so panel beaten by his expectations of women that he looked at her and saw consent.

Maybe you disagree. Maybe you think words have the same value out of anybody's mouth, but if you do think that, at least do what our ideal of rational debate demands and question whether you might be mistaken. Too many studies to count have established that the same action can look different depending on who does it. When women occupy exactly half the airtime of a classroom or panel discussion, the other people in the room will feel dominated and will believe that women have unfairly taken up most of the available airspace;[13] when women and men read the same weather forecast out loud, the men are far more likely to be thought of as showing "expertise";[14] when young black men try to cut the chains off a bicycle, onlookers will immediately phone the police, but when young white women do the same thing, passersby will offer to help with the bolt cutter.[15] Why wouldn't words, too, look different depending on who says them? And if you've never seen that happen, might that reveal more about what you see than about what is actually happening?

We built our landscape of public debate on the premise that words were tools that anybody could use and that the clash of ideas would help us change each other's minds and bring us closer to the truth. But what if it turns out that discourse itself is as vulnerable to power imbalances as the problems we are trying to solve with it? Weeks of twisting, unproductive conversations with catcallers taught me to be skeptical of the idea that lays the bedrock for our ideal of persuasion: the idea that words have standardized value. If the very bedrock of our ideal is shaky, what else might we have wrong about how to rationally change our minds?

chapter two

Faith; or, George Michael Was Wrong

There is no species of
reasoning more common, more
useful, and even necessary to
human life, than that which is
derived from the testimony of
men.
—DAVID HUME

> That's not a reliable source.
> — CARDI B

Missy and Dylan would sooner move to Siberia than move out of each other's sentences.

"Did you tell her the—"

"No, not yet, I—"

"So it was a couple years ago, and—"

"It was just after you'd—"

"Oh, yeah, that's right, okay, it was—"

It was only a few years ago, is what they're lining up to explain, that Dylan left the sect he now calls a cult.

Getting people to change their minds about religious sects like this is so difficult that years ago concerned loved ones could purchase the services of self-styled mind changers who would kidnap the believer, deprive them of food, and handcuff them until they rejected certain religious edicts. It was known as "deprogramming," and it just about writes its own satirical headline: "Hard-Minded Rationalists Call for Brainwashing 'Just This Once.'" But Dylan pulled off the change kidnap-free.

Dylan was born into his sect and raised by parents who were strict believers. The sect claims to be an offshoot of Christianity—though Dylan now thinks ordinary Christians should feel besmirched by this—and by the time Dylan was twenty he had spent much of his life reading the Bible and attending scripture and worship sessions, always surrounded by the sect's elders and other believers. He knew ex-members said terrible things about the sect, but he knew better than to believe them, or to even Google the sect's name. He knew you weren't supposed to.

To get a sense of the magnitude of Dylan's mind change, it helps to know what some members of the group believe. The apocalypse is coming. The apocalypse is coming. Actually, the apocalypse was forecast for a generation ago, but the date is different now. There is a revealed truth only known to the all-male governing body. But that truth changes, and the new truth is unveiled in personalized revelations made only to members of that governing body. Believers who break the rules can and should be shunned completely, including by their partners and the people who raised them. Nonbelievers should be converted; the more time believers spend proselytizing, the better. Certain medical treatments should be rejected even when they prevent grotesquely painful deaths. No sex before marriage, no drinking, no smoking, no drugs. No privately formulated interpretations of scripture. If you feel you might be gay or bisexual, you shouldn't ever act on those feelings. Association with nonbelievers is a "danger." Also, Smurfs are a problem. No Smurfs. The details are hazy, but they're thought to be possessed.

"I always believed. Those were my beliefs. I just didn't understand how twisted they were....I was probably never *not* indoctrinated."

It has now been nearly three years since Dylan changed his mind, and he's talking to me from his porch surrounded by domestic normalcy: his wife, Missy; his kids; his yappy dog. He is an earthy kind of guy with a voice full of gravel and a southern twang so unhurried that whole geological eras could fit inside his pauses. His laughs start with seismic rumbles, his hands are the size of shovels, and if he's earthy, then his kids are tiny moons, tumbling in orbit circles around him with their giggle-shrieks. He is so calm and self-reflective in conversation that you find yourself forgetting he used to be just like the believers he's describing, convinced of the apocalypse and utterly resistant to any evidence to the contrary.

It's easy to look at people who believe what Dylan used to and feel they must be making some deep mistake in their cognitive habits (subtext: the kind of mistake *we* would never make). I remember one rainy day at high school when a substitute teacher stuck for ideas about how to fill a health education class decided to play us a documentary about former cult members, presumably in a moment of amnesia about how cruel thirteen-year-olds can be. As we watched interviews with former believers, it wasn't long before the class was in stitches. *They thought WHAT?*

What, precisely, is the mistake that we schoolkids were so confident we couldn't make? What is the glitch in these people's reasoning we should correct if we want them to be more rational?

One simple answer is that Dylan unknowingly broke a simple rule about *when* to believe anything: he believed the things people told him, mainly because he'd been told them.

Maybe that's irresponsible. "The floating of other men's opinions into our brains makes us not a jot more knowing," wrote John Locke. Perhaps in our classroom knee-slapping we thought the same thing: we would never be foolish enough to believe what other people told us simply because they'd said it. We would see the evidence before believing anything, thank you very much.

It's a tempting story. But it's not at all right.

"Did you consciously think to yourself, *I'm gonna change this guy's mind?*"

"Yes. Absolutely. I made a five-year plan."

Missy is the kind of person who'd sound exactly right if she called you "honey." She is maternally brisk, no-nonsense, and few words get away from her without some sort of emphasis. At first Missy puttered about in the background as I spoke to Dylan, but since they see sentences as a collaborative exercise, she eventually tired of delivering her bits from several feet away and came over to join us.

"I could not describe, like, the minute I met him, the minute that I saw him...I just knew. There was something about him. It was like a magnet."

Missy had met Dylan when she took a job at the restaurant he worked at waiting tables. She wasn't a member of his sect, and not because she'd never had the chance to be.

"My family were members when I was young, just coincidentally. And my sister was born very sick. I'm the oldest, so when my mother was in the hospital [having] my baby sister, I was with her."

Also with Missy's mother, she says, was a group of believers whose job it is to accompany unwell members of the sect to the hospital. The sect says these groups knowledgeably interact with physicians about which treatments believers may receive, but Missy thinks they function like religious mobsters, muttering that it'd be a shame if something happened to your salvation. Just after she gave birth, Missy's mother was told that her newborn daughter might very well die without one of the treatments the sect proscribes. She faced a choice: accept the treatment and lose her own place in salvation, or refuse it, as her faith demanded, and risk her daughter's life.

"I was there, I saw it. When she signed the paper stating that she would accept [treatment] for my newborn baby sister, the elders, the wives, they all literally turned around, and they went away. They *left* her. They left her in the hospital, an hour away from her home, alone, with a dying baby. My sister survived, no doubt due to that treatment, but . . . they just left her. They abandoned her."

A believer who breaks an edict like this is usually cut out: the church will not allow them to participate in its rituals, and its members will no longer have contact with them. Being shunned spreads like a pathogen: if you speak to someone who has been cut out, you too can be cut out, as can the people who then speak to you, and so on outward in ever-larger concentric circles of snubbing. Missy's mother never saw those believers again. And she never changed her mind about whether they were right to leave her.

"She had this huge Catholic Bible, and when I was like eleven or twelve, being a sneaky, snoopy kid, I liked to look through it, because it had pictures. And inside of it I found a letter that my mother had written to God, saying, 'I understand that what I was taught was the truth, and I'm hoping that I'll be resurrected, and I can try again after Armageddon.' Even to this day, my mother believes what they believe."

Missy and Dylan started dating soon after they met. She liked how gentle he was; he liked how caring she was. But when Dylan told Missy he was a member of the sect, Missy thought: *Seriously?* Against all her predictions and in spite of her priorities, she had found herself in love with someone who, just like her mother, believed what they were told.

Would you believe something just because other people had told you it was true? The usual answer is most certainly not, and how very dare you for asking. It's the grown-up version of that maternal chorus "If your friends jumped off a cliff, would you do that too?" Here in the well-lit landscape of responsible belief, we don't just accept things on other people's word. We independently check the evidence for something before believing it.

If that's right, one rule about how to change your mind says, "Don't believe things just because someone tells you them." So far, so plausible, but take a look at how many of our perfectly ordinary beliefs turn out to violate this seemingly simple rule: whether it will rain tomorrow, what anyone else's name is, when the next bus is due, where Machu Picchu is, who crossed the Rubicon, how much the US dollar is worth, what shape Africa is, what Abraham Lincoln said at Gettysburg, how cold it is in Antarctica, why the sky is blue, what's inside an atom, what kind of day your coworker had, what's true about vaccines, what's true about climate change—the list quickly gets out of hand and rolls away like unspooling string.

How much of this list do we have perfectly good beliefs about? Most of it. But how much of it have we independently experienced the evidence for? Not a whole lot. I do not need to see the gruesome sight of my own organs to believe what a surgeon tells me about them, and though I have beliefs about which creatures live at the bottom of the ocean, I do not need to set foot in a pressurized container and descend into a hellscape of nightmare fish with lights on their heads just to check those beliefs. I can just believe what people tell me. And that seems a fine way to believe things. When I said I had beliefs about all those things, you didn't read that and think, *Well, you shouldn't*—did you? That sounded like a perfectly acceptable way to structure my cognitive landscape.

It's strange, then, that the "don't believe what you're told" rule is so popular in public consciousness and that "taking someone's word for it" can be shorthand for "being gullible." Even the Royal Society, the world's oldest learned society, chose *Nullius in verba* as its motto: "Take no man's word for it." Today, popular scientists pride themselves on trusting evidence rather than what people say, as though what people say could not itself be evidence. And often in discussing allegations of sexual misconduct, we hear commentators dismiss cases as "he said, she said," as though *what* they said makes no recommendations about what to believe. I truly do not know how this became so widespread when it takes two seconds' reflection to realize how many of our beliefs are rooted in testimony. Perhaps it's part of our fondness for myths of rugged isolation; perhaps we like to spin ourselves the fiction that our belief system, like our money and our success, was wrought entirely without outside help.

But whatever its origins, this attitude to responsible belief is totally unstuck from at least three hundred years of rich and complex philosophy, where the question is no longer *whether* testimony can ground knowledge, but *when*, and *how*. G. E. M. Anscombe—who was so prodigiously good at philosophy that Ludwig Wittgenstein chose her to translate his works and be the executor of his literary estate, despite his general policy of falling silent when women entered his lectures until they got the hint and left—put the central question thus: "We know about Caesar from the testimony of ancient historians, we even have his own writings! And how do you know that those are ancient historians, and these, works of Caesar? You were told it. And how did your teachers know? They were told it." In the face of a question like "How do you know Caesar existed?" Anscombe wrote, "one would have to ask: 'What am I allowed to count as evidence, then?'"[1]

The answer to that question is an entirely separate rabbit hole, as is the question of whether testimony counts as evidence. Opinions are divided. Scottish Enlightenment figure David Hume, to whom Anscombe was responding, thought that our reliance on testimony was a sort of inference "derived from no other principle than our observation of the veracity of human testimony, and of the usual conformity of facts to the reports of witnesses."[2] Against Hume, more recent philosophers—like Australia's prolific C. A. J. Coady—have argued that testimony is a basic way of accessing knowledge, as ground level as perception, and that, in Coady's words, "our trust in the word of others is fundamental to the very idea of serious cognitive activity."[3] Whatever testimony turns out to be, there are questions around how we should treat it. Which way does the default run: Is it that, without reasons not to, we are entitled to believe what we're told? Or are we entitled to believe what we're told as long as we have positive reasons to?

Whatever the rules about when we can believe what we're told, it's hard to dispute that sometimes we can. Seen in the right light, there is something deeply moving about this: it means that we owe much of the vast progress of human enlightenment to the simple fact that we can talk to each other.

And it means that the problem in how Dylan structured his beliefs has to be more complicated than "believing what you're told."

Faith; or, George Michael Was Wrong

So what was it? *Something* was awry. Dylan's beliefs kept a seriously respectful distance from the truth: he believed hellfire was on its way, that the elders around him heard directly from God, that it was his moral duty to shun people who broke the rules. His beliefs tangled in contradictory loops instead of dovetailing into mutual coherence: orthodoxies changed regularly, the apocalypse date kept shifting, and he was convinced of the elders' omnipotence despite their ever-changing revealed truths—were the last guys wrong or not? Any way of thinking that could produce this much labyrinthine wrongness has to have gone wrong somewhere.

It's worth finding out precisely where. Many of us will someday find ourselves in something like Missy's position, trying to talk the people we love out of believing—against all the evidence—what someone powerful is telling them. If we do not understand the structure of our loved ones' beliefs in situations like these, our attempts to change them may well fail.

Missy tried to change Dylan's mind for five years. They moved in together and got engaged not long after they met. Missy was certain she could see through to the man Dylan would be without the sect and certain she wanted to be with that man. She did not, though, want to spend her life with a member of his sect. So the only possible option was to get Dylan to change his mind. But she didn't tell Dylan she wanted him to leave. She knew he might walk away if she revealed the depth of her contempt for the sect.

Instead, she let herself be introduced as a new partner who was open to being baptized. She went to meetings with Dylan; she prayed and clasped hands and sang the songs; she furrowed her brow and took notes in scripture study.

"Most of my notes said stuff like 'WTF,' 'Are you freaking kidding me?' and 'This is BS.' So if they had looked any closer they would have seen all of my writing going 'That's not true' and 'That's not what the Bible says.'"

But they didn't look any closer. They were treating her just like any other new recruit. It's only now that Dylan realizes exactly what that meant.

"She would start to study, and there was lots of love and positive comments. We would get invited to do a lot of things. And then she would back off and stop studying, and it was like turning a faucet off. Just nothing. That was intentional on her part, to show me what love-bombing looked like."

Sometimes Missy would be more explicit and try to argue Dylan out of one of the sect's arbitrary rules.

"Believers say they can't have their children play sports with other children, and I would say, 'Why not? If all of your community is only [believers], that's a pretty cultlike thing to do.' And he's just like, 'Missy, it's not a cult.'"

"Most of the time it just got brushed off," he explains, "or pushed to the back of my mind. I just put it on a shelf. I think it took a lot longer than she was expecting."

Hairstyles changed; holidays came and went. They had children, plural. Missy took a new job in health care, working with people as they prepared to die. She lived surrounded by believers, and every day for years she pretended she was still making up her mind. Every now and then she did private tests to see if Dylan was getting any closer to wanting out.

"I'd say, 'There are [believers] who are moving to countries where the [conversion] need is greater. How do you feel about maybe taking the kids and going to Central America?' And he's like, '*Yes!* I want to move to Central America. We'll have enough [money] for the year.' And I was like: *Holy shit. I am so screwed.* Because I did *not* want to go be a missionary in Central America. I was just trying to figure out where his mind-set was."

If this makes it sound like Missy was on a slick double-agent mission to secure her man and get out with the suitcase full of cash, it's worth saying: it wasn't fun.

"He would take me to their conventions, and I would sit there and literally cry for three days straight. I would have tears streaming down my face. The talks at these conventions are disturbing—they say things that you or I [would be] appalled with."

Once, a woman got onstage to speak about her son's decision to leave the sect.

"She said that it's been hard to not speak to her own son, but it's just like having a child that's dead. I got up and I slammed my chair, and I walked out. There are people that *actually* lose children. And they were gushing over her like she was a saint. It was horrible."

Missy had made a concerted effort to be kind to the believers. Even she doesn't totally know whether that was strategic or just part of who she is: she likes being the friend
who helps you on moving day or brings you freezable meals
if you're sick. There was one elder she still thinks of as a genuine friend: Matthew, a kindly older man whose family developed a fondness for Missy's pink lemonade and cupcakes. A
little ritual formed where she'd bake for their family events,
and her kids would play with his. "I really cared for him," she
says a little ruefully.

But the other elders did not easily forget incidents like the
chair slamming, and, as the years passed and Missy's "poten-
tial interest" in being baptized never quite materialized into
an actual baptism, they made it clear that their Missy fondness barometers had dropped to cool toleration.

Dylan's parents, too, were as strict in their beliefs as they'd
ever been and were not pleased that he had settled down with
someone who was not a fully fledged believer. When Missy
unexpectedly miscarried, Dylan's mother told her, "It's for the
best."

"We've been together seven years," Missy laughs, "and
they've been trying to divorce us for seven years."

"So why did you stick it out, when it was so hard, and
there were so few indications that Dylan was going to change
his mind?" I wanted to know.

Missy is silent for a minute, as though it's been a long time
since she remembered that she could have walked away.

Faith; or, George Michael Was Wrong

"I spend a lot of time with people in very dark times of their lives. If I have to go to the hospital and be with someone as they're getting ready to pass, that's important to me. I gave them my word that I would be there, that they wouldn't be alone. I keep my word. It was hard; I'm not going to act like it was easy. I've never been so hated in my life. But [when we got married], I told him I would be there for him, and I meant it. I gave my word."

But progress had stalled. Five years after Missy started trying to change Dylan's mind, he was no closer to wanting to leave. In hindsight, it's clear why: Missy was focusing on *what* Dylan believed, while Dylan was focusing on *who*. To some extent this is perfectly normal; you can't believe what you're told unless there's a person doing the telling. Our beliefs about what happened at the Rubicon lean on historians; our beliefs about what happened at the meeting yesterday lean on our colleagues; your belief that Dylan and Missy even exist leans on me. But Dylan's faith in his elders was such that he almost didn't care what the content of his beliefs was; what mattered to him was that he believed what his elders said. So Dylan did not need to lose his faith in what his elders were saying; he needed to lose his faith in *them*.

As Missy and Dylan rolled into their sixth year of life in the sect, Matthew the Only Good Elder, appreciator of Missy's cupcakes and lemonade, wasn't looking too good.

"Matthew was up onstage giving a talk. And looking at him, I saw very indicative signs of an impending heart attack.

So I went to his wife after the meeting, which was completely out of my boundaries. But I really liked Matthew a lot. I went to his wife, and I said, 'Has Matthew been feeling okay? It just seems like there's something going on with his heart.' She said he had been really busy and had been complaining of fatigue a lot, and I said it might just be a good idea to get it checked out."

It turned out Missy had been the first among them to accurately predict oncoming doom, and not the trumpets-and-ascension kind that Matthew specialized in, but the altogether quieter kind that simply blocks off a ventricle.

"The doctor said he missed having a heart attack—that going in was the best thing for him, that it protected him from that heart attack. Matthew came up to you, didn't he, Dylan? And he said, 'Missy's pretty observant, isn't she.'"

Missy's intervention had saved his life. Matthew had children and a wife he would have left behind and was still at the age where his sudden death would have seemed like an injustice. Too circumspect to make a to-do, Matthew resumed his duties as an elder, and Missy and Dylan returned to their domestic normalcy with Matthew's family, baking and visiting, chatting about the day's religious service. But in some silent way they felt more deeply connected to him in the way you do when mortality whistles by and you all say, "Did you hear *that*?"

Dylan kept worshipping. Missy went back to her life of pretending to tolerate their views.

Months later, Dylan got an unexpected phone call from Matthew.

"He said, 'What's [Missy's] disconnect? Why won't she [get] baptized?' He said she was a danger to the congregation. I asked if she'd done anything wrong, and he said that because she was so nice, and so well liked, that made her a danger to the congregation. He said that his family wasn't allowed to have contact with us anymore, because she wouldn't start studying [scripture] again."

Missy interjects: "He said, 'You [have] to choose between your wife and God.'"

"She had been *so* nice, throughout the years...She went out of her way, like if someone was sick, she would cook for them. She was always—with nothing in return, too, that's just not how we operate. So with him talking about her like that—"

It's clear that Dylan sees this as the big turning point, the bright light he could not look away from, so I wanted to be sure I understand his indignation.

"This is someone who owed Missy his life?"

"I don't look at it as saving his life," Missy demurs, but Dylan won't have it.

"*I* did," he says. "I looked at it as at the very least preventing a heart attack. And so for him to be the one to call me and say these things...That conversation totally changed every viewpoint that I held. I think that conversation happened on a Monday night, and the last meeting I've ever been to was that Wednesday."

The evening after he spoke to Matthew, Dylan Googled his sect for the first time in his life.

"I found, like, all apostasy YouTubers and the ex-members' communities online. I'd just always been taught that these people are out to hurt current believers."

"He told me that when he started looking at them, it was like his stomach felt scared," Missy adds.

"[But] I couldn't have been further from the truth about them. They genuinely wanted to help me and other people who were trapped."

"He started spending a really long time in the bathroom, where he would read on his phone," Missy remembered. "And I [was] like: *Uh-huh. And so it begins.*"

Over the next forty-eight hours Dylan read everything he could find and started giving himself permission to wonder: What *did* explain all that apocalypse date shifting? Why were elders allowed to own stocks and bonds when it was considered idolatry for other believers to do the same thing? What did all that punitive shunning do to people psychologically? Australia's Royal Commission into Institutional Responses to Child Sexual Abuse had just investigated the sect, finding it has not adequately dealt with members accused of pedophilia. It didn't exactly halt Dylan's cascading loss of confidence.

When Dylan told Missy he was having doubts, she didn't pretend to be disappointed.

"I was in what I feel is a unique situation," Dylan explains. "Because [Missy] wasn't in...it was different to what a lot of other people go through. I didn't have to worry about staying hidden or having to wake her up. The [only other] people that I cared about were my parents, and I was just okay realizing that sooner or later I wouldn't have a relationship with them."

Two days after speaking to Matthew, Dylan went to worship for the last time.

"Missy always told me they always speak in the same monotone, but I was seeing it for the first time. I was just sitting there looking around, and I started realizing I was there with a bunch of robots. It was like being in a movie."

"So it wasn't gradual?" I asked him.

"No, no. It was like turning off a faucet. Just—gone."

He went home and told Missy he wanted to leave. They took a picture together to mark the occasion, beaming, side by side. Dylan's smile is so wide that his eyes disappear into Vs of joy set into his face. He posted it to one of the apostasy forums he'd found and captioned it, "My wife is without doubt the most beautiful and talented person I know."

A lot of people ask whether Dylan feels betrayed by the revelation that Missy had been feigning her initial openness to his beliefs.

"There's times when she'll say something about how I used to believe that still gets under my skin, but...she's extremely talented. She knew it was a cult; she just loved me enough to try to help me. One thing she said to me before

71

all this happened was, 'At the end of the day, if you do something like [smoke a cigarette], you could be shunned, and you would lose *everyone* around you. But no matter what you do, you won't lose me.'"

It's possible, of course, that Dylan's instant-feeling conversion had been years in the making. Perhaps Missy's doubt and questions had been bubbling away like lava underneath the crust of Dylan's conscious mind until one day all that molten uncertainty belched upward in a volcanic flare. Philosopher-psychologist William James, brother of novelist Henry James—though he probably tired of the comparison— and the first person to teach psychology in the United States, spent much of his life studying the psychology of these sorts of "conversion" moments. A religious man himself, his main interest was in spiritual conversion, but he also studied consciousness alterers like amyl nitrite and peyote, becoming the first to say out loud what most of us only dare think: only on nitrous oxide did he see what Hegel was getting at. In a series of lectures in 1901–1902, titled *The Varieties of Religious Experience*, James wondered whether moments of sudden revelation might not be as sudden as they seem: that what looks to us like an "instantaneous" conversion may in fact be the product of "subconscious incubation," an "explosion, into the fields of ordinary consciousness, of ideas elaborated outside of those fields in subliminal regions of the mind."

It's hard for Dylan to speculate about whether this is right. The "subliminal" is difficult enough for ordinary people to access under ordinary circumstances, but Dylan's circumstances were in the proper sense extraordinary. He has trouble remembering "from the inside" what it was like before he changed his mind. He remembers facts, but the feeling of being a believer is a little harder to muster. It's as though he can no longer speak in the first person about who he was before. He talks about "that person" instead, as though his mind change severed him so completely from his previous self that all he can do now is guess about that person's feelings by forensically reconstructing them from the evidence trail of his behavior.

Whether James's model is right about Dylan's moment of conversion or not, Dylan is confident that his phone call with Matthew yanked a thread that unraveled all the others.

"It seems like you had to change your mind about the people, almost, before you could change your mind about their religious beliefs," I say to him.

"Yes. Yep. You're absolutely right. And that personal betrayal hurts far more than the religious betrayal."

We still don't have an answer to the important question. What was the big flaw in Dylan's belief system?

Here's what I think happened.

I said earlier that it's perfectly ordinary to believe what people tell us and that it's perfectly ordinary to do so in part because we trust the people who do the telling. The bare-minimum version of this involves thinking that those people have access to more evidence than we do, like when we trust strangers who tell us where the train stations are in a city we're exploring, or immunologists who tell us about vaccines, or deep-sea divers who tell us about the ocean floor.

But Dylan's belief structure lets us see a version of taking someone's word for it that goes beyond the bare minimum. In this case, the thought isn't just someone has more evidence than us, but that their belief-formulation systems are on the whole better than ours, because they have attributes or abilities or ways of reasoning that we don't.

This way of accepting someone's word can be strikingly unaffected by the boundaries of credibility. Teachers and university lecturers are familiar with the strange habit students have of coming to them for advice about relationships or career choices or political leanings, as though expertise in one area bleeds across all the others. Dan Ariely is a behavioral economist and academic at Duke University who suffered burns over 70 percent of his body in his youth. "I'm often surprised by how much people confide in me," he wrote in his book *Predictably Irrational*, telling the story of a student who had come to him for advice about which of two boyfriends she should choose. "I think it's partly due to my scars, and to the obvious fact that I've been through substantial trauma."[4]

But why should this matter? It's not as though the student seriously believes Ariely's burns give him insight or evidence about which boyfriend to choose. Instead, it's that there is something about Ariely—he may think it's his burns, but as someone who isn't him, I'm allowed to say it might also be his approachable, unflustered, wry demeanor—that makes the student think his whole way of reasoning might be worth deferring to: that he might have ways of processing this dilemma that she doesn't. She thinks of him as wise. Her hope is that she could take a given input, turn it over to his mind, and trust the output.

This isn't necessarily a bad thing. When someone shows certain traits in their area of expertise—like attention to detail, or the capacity to weigh different sorts of value, or a detached and clinical gaze—it's not completely ludicrous to imagine those traits might generalize. Many of us have been shaped and improved by precisely this way of trusting people.

But here is one difference between what most of us do in these ordinary cases and what happened in Dylan's. When you or I trust our "wise" grandparents or teachers because we think they are wiser than us, there is a kind of "training wheels" structure at play: it's supposed to help us for the time being, stabilizing us and helping us move forward on our own, but we are allowed—encouraged, even—to think that one day we'll be able to reason without help. If we have chosen the right people to think of as wise, they will be excited to see us develop our own ability to think independently. Witness the way that parents (good ones, anyway) start out as the Alpha and Omega of their infant children's beliefs but eventually, around the adolescent years, encourage their children to develop their own priorities and values. If our credibility role models are as wise as we think they are, they will not want us to rely on their word to the exclusion of all other ways of reasoning, and they will not want to be our only strategy for thinking about the world and our place in it.

In Dylan's case, though, he was explicitly discouraged from ever taking the training wheels off. He had grown up thinking his elders and scriptural leaders were better, wiser, and more enlightened than he was, not just because they had access to more evidence, but because without them he would never be able to access the truth. This was the structure embedded by their claim to revealed truth: their status as "sole holder of knowledge" meant that taking their word for it wasn't *an* option for Dylan; it was the *only* option. They alone had the traits or abilities that meant God had chosen them, and they alone had the evidence. On both counts, Dylan was taught from his childhood that any conclusions he reached by himself would necessarily be less informed than theirs. They built their claim to knowledge by robbing him of his, in effect ransoming his ability to access truth to his willingness to keep deferring to them.

If Dylan had ever disagreed with them, the sect would have replied that the very fact of his disagreement was proof that he was worse at reasoning than they were. Remember that believers are discouraged from even interpreting scripture on their own and that the primary justification the sect uses to discredit people who have left is to point out that they have left. The *desire* to have independent thoughts functions as evidence that those thoughts are not to be trusted.

Faith; or, George Michael Was Wrong

The natural consequence of this kind of structure is that the "inferior" thinkers internalize the lesson, while the system of strict punishments and shunning reinforces it. Once, in his early twenties, Dylan had been found drinking and smoking by members of the sect. The sect responded by meting out a watered-down version of the shunning that Missy's mother had experienced. He would be restored to his previous standing only if he was sufficiently penitent and wrote a series of official letters asking for the mercy of the people above him. In the meantime, he was cut out. His family was not supposed to speak to him. His best friend saw him in a supermarket, turned on his heel, and walked away without a word. Instead of asking what kind of belief system could conclude that this was an appropriate way to respond, Dylan agreed. He wrote his letters, a lot of them, all streaked with an awful purgatorial pleading for approval. No wonder he internalized the lesson that he did not deserve to reason for himself when independent thoughts like "I'll have a few drinks" had cost him so much. As long as he was in their community, the only way he could be seen as someone capable of reason—or even see himself that way—was to think and do as his elders did.

And no wonder Missy's attempts to present him with mind-changing argument and evidence didn't gain much traction in his mind. It's no good throwing someone a life buoy if the ocean has convinced them they can't float.

Dylan is not a worse thinker than the rest of us; he is not cognitively broken, and he was not delusional. He is someone.

who began life using perfectly ordinary strategies like believing what people told him and thinking that some people were globally wiser than him. Neither of these was the problem: the problem was that none of the people he trusted encouraged him to develop his own ability to reason or even treated him as though he might have had such an ability. Taking people's word for something is supposed to make us better knowers, not condemn us to a self-justifying loop of deference where the people we defer to encourage us to defer to them on the question of whether we should keep deferring.

The good news, for Dylan and for those of us who lose loved ones to this kind of snare, is that once credibility spreads across multiple areas, a failure in one area can become a failure in all. Dominoes don't mind which direction they topple in. Dylan had grown up believing that elders like Matthew were wiser than him in that all-areas kind of way. So when Dylan heard Matthew describe Missy as slippery and dangerous, contradicting all Dylan's firsthand evidence that she was kind and loyal and loving, at last he saw that Matthew could get things wrong and that he, Dylan, could reach conclusions of his own. He had seen Missy raise their children, take care of people as they died, support him when everyone else in his life would not speak to him for violating the sect's rules. He had seen her care for elders' families and throw herself into a community with kindness and cookies when they had treated her with increasing suspicion and hostility. He was simply confident: Missy was a good person, so Matthew must be wrong. "I just could not fathom why anybody wouldn't want to have her in their life," Dylan says. "She's just such a genuine person." And if Matthew could be wrong about Missy, why not about God, or the nature of the universe?

Dylan was out. That didn't mean he was "in" anything else.

For months afterward his legs felt leaden, like the weight of his lifelong mistakes had been smelted into boots he had to wear around all day every day. He no longer seriously thought that Armageddon was on its way, but that didn't mean he lost the dread in his stomach. He no longer thought there was anyone "up there" who cared what he did with his days, but that didn't extinguish his instinct for prayer. He no longer accepted the teachings against apostasy, alcohol, or medical treatment, but his palms still sweated when he watched YouTube videos from other sect leavers. And the guilt—the guilt unfurled in him like black ink blooming in water. He felt like crying for no reason; his pulse would quicken when he thought of his elders. With terrible regularity, he found himself wanting to die.

"For the first time in my life, it felt like, I found myself knowing absolutely nothing...What kind of person am I going to be, now I don't have any beliefs? Am I still going to be a good person? Am I still worthy of my wife and family?"

Slowly, he reconstructed a self and a value system out of the debris. He's started trying to help other people leave the sect: he tells his story in online apostasy communities and to people he used to know, trying to show believers that it is possible to have a fulfilling life outside. So far, three people he and Missy knew from his sect have followed their lead and left, and hundreds have commented on Dylan's online stories with questions about what it's like to leave.

He took his religious devotion and secularized it, exercising his faith and love through his wife, children, and community. He got a dog. His parents are still in the sect, but his father has agreed to hear his doubts about their teachings.

Many of us have tried, as Missy did, and as Dylan does now, to persuade our loved ones using facts that seem not to have the same purchasing power in our interlocutors' minds as they do in ours. Perhaps in these situations it's worth wondering whether trust of some authority figure is driving our loved ones' beliefs—and whether the credibility they afford them has moved from the ordinary to the sinister. Does their authority figure have a vested interest in denying them access to evidence or an opportunity to reason for themselves? Does their authority figure conflate being questioned with being disrespected? Do they behave as though *not* trusting them is in itself proof of intellectual rot? Do they hint or explicitly claim that they have special "inside" information?

The problem here is not with structuring our beliefs around what we're told. That, by itself, can be moving to behold: we have to see each other as sources of something important for the whole thing to work: it could be knowledge, or authority, or the ability to think for ourselves, but whatever it is, there is something unifying about the mutual recognition required for the communication of knowledge. Done right, it can add up to what Edward Craig, in his work on social epistemology, called "that special flavour of situations in which human beings treat each other as subjects with a common purpose."[5]

The problem is instead with the special odiousness it requires for anyone to take that phenomenon and turn it into a tool of subjugation, using it to mark themselves off as the truth havers and elevate themselves from the people who must rely on them, encouraging the "lesser" thinkers to stop seeing themselves as even capable of accessing the truth. It is an assault on more than just our ways of thinking—it is an assault on some dimension of our moral standing, and it requires a special sort of megalomania to demand obedience in thought as well as in action. Partners who convince their other halves they cannot think for themselves, political leaders who encourage their population to think that they alone hold the truth, and the apparently infinite variations of religious fundamentalism are all cases where the fact that someone believes in the word of an authority figure means they are less likely to see themselves as a source of truth. No wonder these sorts of views, like Dylan's, are so hard to shift with persuasive dialogue alone: the whole structure of the belief we are trying to dismantle means that we are reasoning with someone who has been convinced they cannot (or need not) reason.

The challenge, then, when our loved ones find themselves trapped in this sort of self eroding system may not be to overturn their beliefs but to overturn the system of deference that generates them.

If this were an easy task, none of us would have lost loved ones to closed-off hierarchical groups. But it's not an easy task. It took Missy more than five years to have an effect on Dylan, and even then luck played its part. In another world or another love story, Matthew's mistrust of Missy might have struck Dylan as yet more evidence that elders were better at thinking than he was. Longer marriages than theirs have been undone by an Iago-like suggestion to one spouse that the other might not be trustworthy. But we do each have our own idiosyncratic and personal confidences that can disrupt an otherwise impermeable system of deferring to other people, acting like a kind of reflective surface for suspicion, so that the people who tried to make us doubt them wind up— finally, blessedly—as the objects of doubt themselves.

This is one of the things that stands out about cases where we need to break deference loops like Dylan's: it may be a case of a persuasive mission where it is completely legitimate to bring in the personal. Ordinarily, it's easy to think that that's bad practice, or the sign of a faltering argument. In Persuasion 101 manuals they tell you to play the ball, not the man. But in cases where someone's deference to another person—or group of people—is near total, then what's at issue is the man. Disrupting that system of deference is part of our mission as much as undermining the actual content of any of the resulting beliefs. If the character of the authoritative people is part of what creates the belief, why not let it play a legitimate part in tearing it down?

Whatever the appropriate strategic moves in cases like these, one thing seems clear: persuasive progress is unlikely if we simply berate our loved ones for having believed what they were told in the first place. It is cosmically bad luck to find yourself in a situation like Dylan's, surrounded by people who take an ordinary belief-forming practice that should function like a ballast and turn it into a strangler vine. If you have been to the Amazon and seen real strangler vines, the thick, sinuous ones that look like braided pythons and constrict a rigid tree so hard it starts to bulge like a trussed ham, you already know the point I'm trying to make in this extended metaphor: those things are terrifying, and if you want to untangle them, you don't just yell at the tree for standing near them in the first place. The tendency to believe what we are told is not *unto itself* the problem.

Dylan says his father won't look at the materials he found online. He doesn't think that's going to change: they are apostate materials, after all. But I can't help asking Dylan, "Do you think there's any chance [your parents] would have a similar conversion?"

There is the world's longest pause. The air is so cold I can see my question hanging in it. A pair of eagles tilt on the breeze, wings bright as sickles.

"I don't know," says Dylan. "Sometimes I think yes."

chapter three

Fake It 'til You Make It and/or Forget Who You Are

Each of us constructs and lives
a "narrative," and this narrative
is us, our identities.
—OLIVER SACKS

This appalling narrative business
of the realist: getting on from
lunch to dinner: it is false, unreal.
—VIRGINIA WOOLF

Alex was a bouncer when he changed his mind about who he was. Or maybe he wasn't a bouncer. Maybe he was only pretending.

That wasn't the right place to start the story.

The right place to start is in the offices of the UK TV station Channel 4 in the year 2000, when "reality TV" still sounded to most people like an oxymoron. *Big Brother* had only two months under its belt, the first of the *Idol* shows was still in development, and Kim Kardashian was some years away from her first velourish and obsequious appearance as Paris Hilton's closet organizer in *The Simple Life*. Reality TV was different then—social media did not yet exist, and *Bridalplasty* and *Jersey Shore* had not yet trained us to expect on-screen "realities" that came with lips and biceps and plot lines that were as shiny and plastic as balloons and just as stretch-marked from overinflation.

Instead, what we got was a spate of programs that filmed ordinary people in slightly peculiar circumstances of being filmed—*Big Brother* filmed people inside a house; *An American Family* simply followed an American family. Alfred Hitchcock once said that if you wanted suspense, you'd put a bomb between two characters and have them talk about the weather. The real insight of those early reality TV formats was that you could film people talking about the weather, and the audience would infer their own bombs: the most excruciating narrative tension you could subject your audience to was just life, where anything might happen. There were no tropes or well-worn plot lines to reassure us that we kind of knew the ending already or that we wouldn't see real failure or mental breakdown onscreen. If we did, what if—god forbid—we were *entertained*? It was a bizarre new genre that was half entertainment and half psychological warfare where neither audience nor participants were quite sure which of them were the combatants.

Two big figures at the forefront of the UK reality TV boom set the stage for our story: executive producer Stephen Lambert, who looks like a turtle tasked with solving a serious crime, and director Mike Warner, who looks like a turtle who has committed a serious crime. They each have shiny bald heads and piercing eyes that presumably see straight into the human condition because they have had a hand in some of the most well-known reality TV formats to date. Lambert's CV includes *Wife Swap*, *Undercover Boss*, *The Secret Millionaire*, and *Gogglebox*, while Warner took the helm of *My Big Fat American Gypsy Wedding* and the "make-under" show *100% Hotter*. Every show reliably pulls off the delicate balance between the bright and the sinister. Warner and Lambert are the Rothkos of reality TV.

In 2000 Lambert came up with a program called *Faking It*, which had a simple setup: each week a participant with an archetypical identity—dressage rider, say, or skinhead, or working-class house painter—would be tasked with learning a skill that jarred with that identity, like boxing, or conducting a symphony orchestra, or creating conceptual installation art. The participant had four weeks to perfect that skill before being sent to a real event full of real professionals in that skill, where they would have to pass undetected by a group of experts who had been asked to spot the imposter. Lambert conceived of the show as a modern-day *Pygmalion*, but in *Pygmalion* we know the ending, while in *Faking It* we had the weekly anxiety of not knowing if the participants would be humiliated on national TV. Warner, meanwhile, was the director in charge of the show's first episode—and of Alex.[1]

Elbow-patched Alex arrived on the program as the toffee-nosed eldest son of an upper-class British family. He was twenty years old and as Oxbridge as it's possible to imagine. If you took Bertrand Russell, bound him in leather, and made him smoke a cigar made entirely of armchairs, you'd still be several cups of tea short of Alex. We meet him for the first time at his family's country home, where he shows us around the grounds and introduces us to Roger, who is a horse.

Alex's task on *Faking It* was to pass as a bouncer at one of London's busiest nightclubs in the middle of the 2000 UEFA European Football Championship. He would have to stand at the door and tell burly, drunk fans that they couldn't come in, and he'd have to do it in a way that meant they slunk away quietly instead of trying to punch him. This was a problem because Alex was five foot six and slight, with a body that kept a respectful distance from any image of athleticism. His manner was no help, either—his perfectly clipped private-school consonants and eager-to-please eyes were obvious artifacts of a life spent very far from rowdy pubs and football. Alex is not deterred: he packs his clothes; says good-bye to his boyfriend, Clinton; bids adieu to Roger; and sets out to fake it.

To help him act the part, the team at *Faking It* matched Alex up with three advisers—kickboxing champion Tony, former police officer and security expert Charlie, and voice coach William—and sent him to spend the month living with Tony on the fifteenth floor of a council housing block in Hackney, East London. Alex has never seen London before, and as his taxi drives toward Tony's flat, he stares out the window with his eyes and mouth wide open. "My god, look at this place. Laundrette—oh my god, there's a—I don't think I've ever seen a laundrette…There's a mattress! There is a *mattress*, on the pavement…I'm going to get beaten, the absolute shit out of me, in this tie. And this jacket. Oh. My. God."

When the taxi pulls up, Tony and Charlie watch from the balcony and shake their heads in disbelief. They show him around, and afterward Charlie looks like someone who's taken a bet on a pomeranian in a fight against a Great Dane. "I do think it's gonna be a hard four weeks for us," Charlie says. "And a very tough four weeks for him."

How do you change your mind about who you really are? Presumably, you start with a view about what your "true" self is like and then go on to repudiate that view, but even that first step turns out to be remarkably difficult, because you have to work out what a "true" self could be. "I've yet to meet anyone who can explain clearly what this 'me-ness' is," writes English philosopher Julian Baggini, who has explored ideas of personal identity. "Although people recognise that they have changed enormously since they were children, most claim that, nonetheless, their sense of 'me-ness' has remained constant."[2]

When Alex arrived on *Faking It*, he thought he knew what his sense of "me-ness" looked like. It was marching him toward a future life in a big country house, going to horse trials, hunting and shooting, taking holidays to Scotland to fish for salmon. But as you've probably guessed by now, that isn't how it worked out. Something about *Faking It* changed Alex's mind about what his "true" self was really like.

How is that possible? What rational cogs are turning for people when they change their minds about who they are? Are beliefs about ourselves even the kind of thing we can be rational about, when *we're* the ones who make those beliefs true?

I had to ask Alex directly.

I found him in Australia, where he now lives—except for the ten days a year when he goes home to see his family. It's been nearly twenty years since the program first broadcast, and he still sounds like the educated Englishman he was on the program, but his vowels have been hammered flat by years in Australia, and he is nowhere near as affably eager to please. He is grounded, and uninterested in seeking approval.

In some way I think I'd expected to *know* him, but when he says he's changed, he isn't lying.

I asked if the show changed his beliefs about himself.

"Did going on the show really change your understanding of who you were?" I ask.

"Yes. Completely," Alex says. "I did a complete and utter 180. After the show—or, after that experience; I don't really look at it as a show anymore—four or five weeks after I got back home to Oxford, I left the UK and came to Australia. I literally dropped everything. I arrived in Australia with a backpack and not much else."

Before that moment, Alex's life had followed a predictable pattern. "I was at [public] school; I went to prep school—I was head of school at both of those. I then became an Oxbridge candidate. I did everything I was supposed to do. I was the good eldest son of the eldest son, and I loved it. And then [the show] was this sort of great chasm that broke that in my mind, and I went, 'Hang on—there's another side to all of this. I don't have to do all those things anymore. I don't have to be someone's son, or brother, or grandson. I can actually be... *me*.'"

I wondered whether Alex might have gone into the program because he secretly hoped for this kind of revelation.

"No, no, I had absolutely no idea what I was getting into," he says. "It was all really weird how it came together in the first place... I was just doing it because it sounded fun—they didn't tell me what it was until I'd signed on the dotted line.

I just knew that it was a 'transformational experience.' I just thought, 'All right, I'll give it a crack,' signed on the dotted line, and then it was all gone too far to turn back, I suppose. So I wasn't going on any mission of self-finding. Because I didn't realize I was lost."

What is going on in this kind of mind change? Do our beliefs about who we are change just like any other belief, or is there some funny footwork we need to do when changing our minds about ourselves, because in that case alone we are both the holders and the objects of the belief?

More pressingly, *how* do we do it? Is it the kind of thing we can be persuaded into? I know dozens of people whose current belief about their "true" self has them endlessly enacting a story that they'd do well to be talked out of, as they take great bong hits of narratives like "I don't deserve love" and "I always mess everything up," and then immediately behave so as to prove that story right. I think everyone knows people like that, or deep down fears they might be one of those people. It would pay to be able to answer the question "Who would we be, if not for who we already think we are?"

One challenge we face in answering this question is that the standard "mind-change" model (think something, get evidence against it) does not fit neatly onto self-to-self cases. What does it mean to have a belief about your true self? What even *is* a true self? If we're to try changing our minds about who we "really are," we'd best have some idea of what that in fact amounts to. It's no good trying to change your own mind—or, worse, someone else's—about something you can't even begin to describe.

One possibility involves understanding the "self" as the center of an autobiographical story—a kind of internal narrator who unifies the past and future into a coherent story told through our own perspective. Of all the available senses of self, from our visual sense of what we look like to our physical sense of where we are in space, this "narrative" sense of self is the one that really matters. Marya Schechtman, a philosopher and neuroethicist who has done considerable work on the question of selfhood, has argued at length for this narrative view: "We constitute ourselves by understanding our lives as narrative in form and living accordingly. Having a narrative, and so being a self…is primarily a matter of keeping track of this [narrative] background and responding accordingly."[3] Indeed, I often hear people speak in ways that connect their sense of self with their sense of an internal story: in the opening pages of his memoir, *Life Itself*, film critic Roger Ebert writes, "I was born inside the movie of my life."[4] Having one's story heard seems to matter for feeling that one's real self has been heard. Conversely, being unable to tell a coherent internal story seems to jeopardize our chances at a coherent self; instead, in psychoanalyst Stephen Grosz's words, "we dream these stories, we develop symptoms, or we find ourselves acting in ways we don't understand."[5]

So how would we debunk the autobiography we have been mentally narrating and replace it with a more accurate one?

The narrative sense of self is all very well, but nobody wants to be spinning fiction. Come too unglued from the facts about who you really are, and your internal narrator won't be a coherent self but a legitimate candidate for being institutionalized. How do we get stories about ourselves, just like every other story that claims to be true, to be open to falsification?

Here we hit the first problem: unlike any other story, our stories about who we really are have the luxury of being able to create their own evidence. Our internal narration about what kind of person we are can become our reason for acting in a particular way; then we act in that particular way and create more supporting evidence for the story about being that particular way, such that the story forms a self-justifying loop turning ever around on itself like an evidentiary Möbius strip. Our habits and thoughts and actions can start to look like independent proof of our internal narrative instead of its artifacts: we forget to check inside our actions for the fingerprints of the story they claim to verify.

Alex, from where he sits now, is especially well positioned to see how internal narrators can tamper with the evidence. "Absolutely. That's absolutely right," he agrees. "I was doing what I should have done, and I loved what I should have done because I should have done it, and then I did it, so I [thought] I should do it some more."

Occasionally, *Faking It* had a contestant who spent their whole month in foot-shuffling self-consciousness. One episode tasked a prim lawyer with becoming a garage MC, and the poor man never quite got over how unlike him it was to rap. Weeks into his training, friends from his old life were still joining him in the studio to gawk at his baggy pants and the way his mentors said "riddim" instead of "rhythm," and he wasn't the only one who played the "this is out of character!" joke for a little too long. Arms-lengthening it was a sort of defense mechanism—if I'm winking and laughing enough to signal that this isn't something my "real" self would do, then *I* can't really fail.

Alex isn't like that. After that first car ride into London, he doesn't ever again make a shtick of giggling for the camera. There are no pantomimes of incredulity when he sees drunk Londoners for the first time; he doesn't go for easy punch lines about his voice sounding out of place. Things get very real when he goes for his first kickboxing lesson. All Tony's male fighters are so much bigger than Alex that it'd be like putting an orca in the same weight class as a hamster, so Tony's girlfriend, Berenice, climbs in the ring with him. As Tony gets them ready, Alex says, "What, we're not role-playing?" Half a second after Tony says "Go!" Berenice hits Alex, hard. Alex goes down, plainly hurt, and it would have been easy for him to defuse his humiliation by doing a self-conscious Basil Fawlty ho-ho for the camera, but he doesn't: they keep fighting, and when Berenice literally shoves him off the mat, he makes no effort to hide or wink at the fact that he is curled up and wheezing. He is not trying to be anything other than what he is: a young man who's been hit in the face and who needs to get a lot better, quickly.

When he goes for lessons with his acting coach, William, he pays careful attention to his instruction in East London grammar, whittling his pronunciation of "Tott-en-ham" down to "Tot'nam" and repeating, "I was, you was, he was, she was, they was, but he weren't." He has his head shaved; he starts walking with more bounce in his knees; he stays in character around the clock and starts filming his video diaries in his new accent.

"So why did you commit so much?" I ask him, trying to find something that might explain his change of mind. Maybe he was secretly trying to shed his old identity all along.

"No, I had never had any of those existential thoughts whatsoever. It just sort of happened," Alex remembers. "I think it helped that [the producers] put me through three-day training"—a crash course so that his final test at a major nightclub wouldn't be flatly illegal. "I'd come from 'qualifications are king,' with uni and GCSEs and A-levels. And I had a piece of paper, and it said I was qualified. That piece of paper was a huge strength, just knowing that I could do it."

The other big help was that somewhere along the way, Tony, Charlie, and William had changed their minds about Alex. Something about his commitment to the role seemed to have won them over, and they accepted him onto that plane of UK male friendship of laugh-shoving each other in the shoulder. Even early on, as Tony and Alex sit in the stands at Arsenal Stadium for a lesson in soccer partisanship, Tony says, "I'm sitting next to a different person to the one that turned up on my doorstep last week." He sounds like nothing so much as a proud dad. "Just knowing that I had the support of actual people who were doormen," says Alex, still proud, "I was buggered if I wasn't going to do it."

But willpower alone never made a plausible bouncer. Alex is still noticeably smaller than everyone else in the profession, and now and then he unknowingly slips back into speaking with consonants as sharp as the crease in his pants. He's maintaining the cover story about being from the inner city, but there's no shortcut to twenty years' worth of inside local knowledge. In one hair-raising scene, a barber who isn't in on the scam asks an in-character Alex what he thought of one of the European Championship football matches, and even now as I watch it I can't shake the fear that Alex is going to flub it. On his first night as a bouncer in a bar, Tony sends him to clear a downstairs area that's due to close. Alex orbits helplessly around the small circles of drinkers, saying, "Excuse me, guys, do you mind just going upstairs now?" Eventually, Tony asks them to move, and the crowd shifts upstairs right away, as fluid and group thinking as a shoal of fish.

"I did some really silly things that I now look back on and think, 'Oh my god, that could have gone so wrong.' There were a couple of things that they didn't show, because they just couldn't. Like 'I'll get a gun. You're the small one I'll remember you. I'll come back tomorrow night, and I'm gonna get you.' I look at it now and I'm like...he *could* have!"

One night the boys take Alex to a strip club for the first time in his life, a proper one with smoke machines where girls in animal-print underwear slither around poles and then around each other in tubs of foam. Alex does his best to not shrink from the debauchery, but afterward, when they're sitting around a table in an all-night café, he looks faintly like a concussed cartoon character with birds circling around his head.

"What about your first exposure to the exposure...of naked ladies, exposing themselves?" asks Tony.

"It was interesting...," Alex replies.

"'Interesting'—now, that's an interesting word...A book's *interesting*," Tony prods him.

"The other reason that I've never been to a strip club is because, um, I'm gay."

Alex is the only person who seems to view this as any sort of big deal.

"The thing is, if you'd come in on day one and said you were gay, me and Tony would have treated you absolutely no differently," says Charlie. "We've had gay doormen work for us before."

"I know that now, cuz I know you now, but I didn't know that when I walked in the door. When I walked in the door, you were both over six foot and just, like, scary...and I didn't want to—"

"You had your prejudice about us," Charlie nods.

"Yeah. To be quite honest, I did."

It's a moment of genuine tenderness in a show about faking, but what nobody remarked on was that Alex had punctuated his every sentence with an upward-inflected "Yeah?," as in, "I know that now, yeah? Cuz I know you now, yeah? But I didn't know that when I walked in the door, yeah?" His East End accent hadn't slipped the whole time.

If changing your mind about who you really are means getting your internal narrator to tell a story that matches the facts better, presumably we need to find the evidence that will let us access that new story.

The problem here is that the only tool we have for doing this investigation is the very thing that stands to be altered or imperiled by the results of that investigation: the so-called narrator at the center of our lives. This raises a question about who does the displacing: Is our "true" self somehow able to narrate itself into existing—or, weirder still, able to *reason* itself into existing? It sounds, to slightly co-opt J. David Velleman's phrase in his work on selfhood, "not just magical but paradoxical, as if the rabbit could go solo and pull himself out of the hat."[6]

On top of this existential magic, we would need a way to work out which of the available evidence really matters and which way it plays. We would need to distinguish between the actions and thoughts and habits that reveal something deeply true about ourselves and the actions and thoughts and habits that we can dismiss as the flotsam of social pressure or the old internal narrative. This is difficult, under the circumstances: we shouldn't trust our internal narrator about which of our actions are in and out of character when the accuracy of our internal narrator is precisely what's in question.

At this point, things are already looking pretty sticky, but there's another, bigger, problem with my question about whether we can rationally work out who we "really" are. I've been speaking about the evidence that ushers out the old internal story and the evidence that ushers in the new story in a way that suggests they are one and the same. To be sure, sometimes it works like this—in cases where the old story is just the exact opposite of the new story. But as a generalizable principle, there's no guarantee that things will work like this. Evidence *against* something is not of itself evidence *for* something else, and falsifying one story doesn't always truthify another. There is a very real possibility that the moments that force us to erase our internal narratives will do just that—erase the narrative—and then call it a day. And if having an internal narrative is so important to having a "self," what's left when the narrative crumbles? What are we in the space between stories?

The night of Alex's final test arrives. He is to man the door at the London Hippodrome, a vast nightclub in Westminster that holds two thousand people inside a space that was once used for circuses. Great bovine crowds of drunken football fans have decided the Hippodrome is their destination on the night England plays Germany in the European Championship: they are riotous, shouting, flag-waving, and slurring, struggling to keep both eyelids raised while insisting they need to be let in. Alex's mentors are watching him via a camera feed in the manager's office. They're laughing but plainly nervous; Alex is not in front of the kind of crowd that treats signs of weakness gently. The production team at *Faking It* has enlisted four experienced doormen to be Alex's "competitors"—each of them, and Alex, takes a turn manning the door, and when all five are finished, the Hippodrome's real-life security team is told that one is an imposter.

"I'd say the imposter was number three."

"Well, I thought the imposter was number one."

"It's a tough choice between number one and number three."

"I'd say three."

Alex was number five—none of the security team catches him. His mentors roar with joy. "It's like seein' your kid walk and talk for the first time, innit!" says Tony, genuinely chuffed. The security team is told that Alex was the imposter. One looks genuinely dumbfounded, almost hurt: "No...really? Well, you got me there then. Honestly?"

It is fist-pumpingly good television. The Rothkos of reality TV have given us such a resounding triumph for such an unlikely underdog that we almost didn't notice it had also given us a scene in a strip club and a rich kid getting hit in the stomach. We got the combination of the upbeat and the sinister that lives in the ordinary. Alex packs his things and tells the camera it's all been marvelous. Roll credits; thanks for playing.

But as Alex sits on the train back to his country house, it is no longer entirely clear that he *has* been playing. His whole manner is visibly different from that of the person he had been when he last saw his family and his boyfriend, Clinton. In the postgame wrap-up on the show, drama coach William says something prescient among all the celebrations: "I think he stopped acting about a week ago."

Almost as soon as Alex got home, he realized his old life wasn't going to stick. He packed a single backpack and got on a plane to Australia. When he first arrived he moved straight to Alice Springs, the town at the center of the Australian desert where the sand is an electric orange and the running water often doesn't. "I went to work almost straightaway—I got a job in regional health working with drug and alcohol issues. I worked for the AIDS Council of Central Australia; I helped run a needle-exchange program for the first three months I was there. And that was purely on the strength of what I'd learnt in the show, because I could handle myself. I was so much more confident of myself and my abilities in that world." A couple of nights a week, he worked as a doorman in one of the local pubs. In Australia he moved free of backstory: he wasn't anyone's son, or anyone's friend from a fancy school, or anyone's anything. "At the time it was like, oh my god, here I am getting introduced to people just as, 'This is Alex.'"

He stayed with Clinton, his boyfriend from before the program. He traveled to Sydney and to Melbourne. I can't give you a simple end-state that describes "just Alex" as neatly as the archetype he had when he arrived on *Faking It*. He didn't stick with his East End identity; he didn't stick in Alice Springs; he didn't stick as a bouncer. There's no three-word description that will make you think, *Oh, I get it*. Even Alex can't quite articulate it.

"I was more able to be me and more able to be open about anything here than I was over there. I was just able to be... more...I was going to say 'more normal,' but it's not more normal; it's just *more*." He's stayed in Australia for the past two decades, letting life go about what he calls its "organic progression."

This is what's so striking about Alex's mind change. The moment in his life when he decided he had been wrong about who he was—the moment when he let go of his old life in England—doesn't seem to have been characterized by seeing the evidence for a new internal story so much as simply not telling the old one. He did not deliberate himself into a new sense of self by starting at first principles or being persuaded that in fact the "real" Alex had a certain set of traits. He just stopped believing and waited to see what would happen.

"This weird thing happened—once or maybe twice every couple of weeks, someone would recognize me in Sydney, from the show in London, and go, 'Oh my god, are you...?' People remember it. It stuck in people's heads, which I think is really cool." He got a suit-and-tie job; he loves his friends' kids; for a while he didn't speak much to his family, but he visits them when he can. "Once a year I go back and just become what I was." It is *his* life, not anyone else's.

In the end, I think Alex's experience shows us just how strange it is to think of changing our minds about ourselves as a rational process like every other. I now think my question about whether we can be persuaded into the "right" belief about our "true" selves is a question that dissolves rather than finds a rational answer. The question rests on the false idea that there is some truth waiting to be discovered and that we can get at it with enough evidence, as though the Alex of today was waiting, dormant, inside the Alex of 2000 and that the right sort of evidence—once the distracting pieces of evidence were put to the side—could have revealed him.

But of course he wasn't. The traits and preferences and perspectives Alex now takes to define himself didn't exist to be discovered when he was wondering who he really was; they were made in and by the decision to walk away. Alex could not have reasoned his way into "truer" beliefs about himself because the truth he was trying to uncover was forged only by his attempt to uncover it.

If there is no "real" self waiting to be found, then it's very hard to understand how we could reason ourselves into seeing it. Maybe truths about ourselves are truths we make, rather than discover. Maybe, in that regard, our relationship to our "true" selves is rather more like the art we make than the truths we discover about the world. One of my favorite authors, Geoff Dyer, spent years working on a book about D. H. Lawrence, and in the end what he wrote was *Out of Sheer Rage*, a Catherine wheel of a book that follows Dyer as he tries to write in Rome, in Mexico, in Oxford, in anywhere that isn't here. It's too hot to write; he needs a book he left behind; he's angry; it's not right:

> I regret that [the book] will not turn out to be the sober, academic study of Lawrence that I had hoped to write but I accept this because I know that, in the future, when it is finished, I won't want it to be any different. I'll be glad that this little book turned out how it did because I will see that what was intended to be a sober, academic study of D. H. Lawrence had to become a case history. Not a history of how I recovered from a breakdown but of how breaking down became a means of continuing.[7]

Dyer discovered what he was writing only by writing it.

Maybe the "true" self, the one we are so keen to have true beliefs about, works like this—such that the hope of trying to reason ourselves into knowledge about it just doesn't work. It is not sitting, pre-formed, waiting for a patient archaeologist to excavate it. If that's right, then no wonder it's so difficult to make a model of "rational belief revision" stick.[8]

L. A. Paul, professor in cognitive science and philosophy at Yale, formulates a similar problem in the book she wrote after years of research into what she calls "transformative experiences" like having a child, or getting a cochlear implant, or joining the military: "If we are to make life choices in a way we naturally and intuitively want to—by considering what we care about, and imagining the results of our choice for our future selves and future lived experiences—we only learn what we really need to know after we have already committed ourselves."[9]

For professor Amia Srinivasan, the challenge here is not whether it is *possible* to be rational about such decisions, but whether it is ethical to approach them rationally. "This is a deep issue," she wrote in her review of Paul's book, "and one that decision theory cannot resolve.... That question has always been for us, not the algorithm."[10] Perhaps the challenge in changing our minds about who we really are, then, is not to rationally persuade ourselves into a new story about who we are but to learn to live for periods of our life without one. This sounds like a deeply frightening prospect, if you think that selves just are—or depend upon—a coherent narrative. But I'm inclined to agree with philosopher Peter Goldie, who argued at length in his aptly titled work *The Mess Inside* that this ideal of a stable self is a mistaken one:

> When we are in the process of revising our deeply valued traits, with which we in some sense identify, we are typically in a state of conflict and confusion. I want to argue that conflict and confusion, even if it can be psychologically very painful, can be a good thing as a necessary part of a psychological progress of profound change in one's values, and in particular changes in one's defining traits, traits with which one identifies... change that can (but need not) lead to personal progress, rather than, as Schechtman claims, to a threat to the survival of the narrative self.[11]

Goldie is well positioned to have nuanced thoughts about personal upheaval; he began life as a banker, changed his mind in his middle age, quit his job, and became a philosopher. He goes on to ask if this conflict and confusion, while it may be troubling, may in fact be truly helpful: "Might it not be... a step—perhaps a psychologically necessary one—in the process of profound personal change, perhaps for the better?"

But life unwritten can also be enormously fun. It is the feeling of taking off on a plane not clear about when or if you'll return, and it was part of what made great TV out of episodes of *Faking It* that ended as successfully as Alex's. You got to watch the childish wonder of people realizing that they *could* behave out of character and that they *were* capable of the very things they had declared they could never do. You got to wonder which identities you might like to try on, what possible senses of self lurk outside the one you currently inhabit, and it was hard not to mist up when people broke through their rigid views of themselves to the joy and the promise in the possibility of life unwritten.

In fact, that's part of what made the whole boom of early reality TV so fun—it *felt* unwritten. For a brief and shining moment, the sheer novelty of seeing normal people on television obscured the fact that we were seeing a version of "reality" that had been panel beaten by writers into coherent plot lines. The moment passed—as more and more reality programs proliferated, we started seeing the same sorts of episode; we started to recognize tropes and predictable plot lines, and we learned the rules of the stories. Once that happened, the genre of reality TV slid into a realm where the whole point is narrative predictability. We have talent quests, and baking programs, and the Kardashians, where we tune in because we want the stories we already know: I'm singing because of the terrible trauma of my childhood; I'm really cutting it fine to get this Victoria sponge to rise; maybe Kourtney and Scott will get back together. Of course, I still watch them, but we've long since lost the weird genreless precariousness of the early programs, that electric sense that anything might happen.

When we live governed by an internal story, the truth is that this story—as much as any story we see on television—has panel beaten the facts into a coherent narrative arc. And some facts get left on the cutting-room floor. A decades-long Harvard study into happiness discovered that people often forget having had aspirations that do not later come to fruition.[12] Researchers in the experiment would ask a fifty-year-old a follow-up question about the ambition they had as a twenty-year-old to become a doctor, and the fifty-year-old would swear there had been a mistake: *I never wanted to be a doctor; that must be someone else's file.* Chekhov's gun is the rule in storytelling that if you introduce a gun in act 1, it had better go off by act 3. These people, editing their own lives for narrative coherence, had done what any decent editor would have done. They saw that the gun did not go off and wrote it out of act 1. This is what we do as narrators—we pull facts out when they're just dead weight, or tension that doesn't resolve.

But, of course, facts themselves don't decide who among them is pulling their weight: *we* do. There is no such thing as "narrative significance" until we have worked out what the narrative is. The sense of having an internal narrator is one thing, but the sense of having a coherent internal narrative is quite another. We can mislead ourselves in our search for the latter, pruning facts for relevance, seeking closure where there is none, retroactively infusing events with significance they did not have.

All of this is to say: there may be good reason to avoid "rationally" reasoning ourselves into new stories about who we are. Life without narrative may turn out to be our only option when we find ourselves wondering, as Alex did, who we really are.

I've said so much about why we might mistrust coherent stories, so let me end this story with three bare facts.

When I spoke to Alex last, he and Clinton were coming up on their nineteenth anniversary, which means that this is the year where they have spent more than half their lives together.

Berenice, the girl who monstered Alex in his first kickboxing lesson, married Tony, Alex's mentor.

Alex was their best man.

chapter four

The Hard Drive and the Camel's Back

Faith is nothing but a firm
Assent of the Mind: which if
it be regulated, as is our Duty,
cannot be afforded to anything
but upon good Reason.
—JOHN LOCKE

Against Locke's philosophy I think
it an unanswerable objection (if
we needed any) that, although
he carried his throat about with
him in this world for seventy-two
years, no man ever condescended
to cut it.
—THOMAS DE QUINCEY

S usie hadn't known John's secret. After she found out, she phoned his mother to say she was filing for divorce, but his mother didn't need an explanation. "It's the babysitting thing, isn't it?"

Susie had met John in a chat room in the early 1990s, back when the Internet made a sound like bagpipes struggling through a snowstorm and computers were huge boxes the pale brownish color of dentures left in tea. John and Susie were both in their early twenties, both single, and even when their only contact was instant messaging, it didn't take long to discover that they were each other's sort of person.

At first Susie thought it wouldn't go much further; he was just some guy from the Internet. But then a cute coincidence made John seem like a real prospect: John's childhood best friend had a sister, and that sister was marrying Susie's first serious boyfriend. Susie still counted this ex as a dear friend, so "I called him, like, 'Guess who I met!'...And he said, 'Do you know, I think you might really like him.'"

Susie's talking to me from her house in Chicago at the end of a winter so sharp it blistered the siding. She has the sunny matter-of-factness of someone who is used to being good in a crisis, which makes sense because she is: she's a social worker for families whose children might die or already have. She is straight-talking, sounds like her sleeves are always rolled up, and hems her sentences with silver linings.

It's the first time she's told this story at length in public, and though it's decades since she first met John, it's clear even now that she's telling a love story. This is act 1, with the cute coincidences and the crackle of what's to come. She makes a little character out of the ex-boyfriend saying "You might really like him" in the conspiratorial eyebrow-waggling tone of a teen at a sleepover.

Susie and John lived in different cities when they met, but one weekend she had a conference in his area, and they arranged to have dinner in person. John was the son of a veteran; he was stoic, self-sufficient, witty. He fit her vision of a partner.

"The thing that struck me was that he didn't play games. Everything seemed out in the open, and I was *so* tired of people playing games. The night we had dinner, I drove home, and I called my mom and said, 'I think I could marry this guy.'"

Four years later, she married that guy. They bought a house; they had a daughter. The love story was supposed to progress to act 2. Except that Susie isn't her real name, she doesn't live in Chicago, and John has been dead for years.

To hear a certain sort of person tell it, you can measure someone's intellectual fortitude or strength of character by their willingness to doubt what they already believe. Think bumper-stickerable maxims like "Wisdom is doubting all certainty." You see a fair number of these slogans if you live anywhere near an intellectual landmark. For me it's Albert Einstein's old house in Princeton, New Jersey, where a stream of memorabilia connects doubt to rationality. "The important thing is not to stop questioning," says a mug. "Question everything," says a T-shirt, truncating slightly to allow for sleeves.

I think part of the vogueish association between doubt and intellectual bravery is owed to the fact that history's doubters have been—there's no other way to put it—cool. So much of our cultural and scientific inheritance is presented as (or maybe is) a story about people daring to doubt, from Galileo to Darwin, to the revolutionary Thomases—both Paine and Jefferson. And if the story of human progress is the story of democratizing doubt, then it's easy to understand why the contemporary faces of that story follow suit, like Clarence Darrow, the lawyer famous for his defense of a teacher prosecuted in 1925 for teaching evolution in Tennessee, who wrote, "I have always felt that doubt was the beginning of wisdom," or Christopher Hitchens, historian and acerbic commentator, who said that our skepticism is "the only thing" that separates us "from other mammals" and that to surrender it "is [a] sinister thing."[1]

There's one remark I hear quoted over and over as a slogan recommending constant doubt; it is Oliver Cromwell's, as he was fighting the Scottish Army loyal to King Charles II in the midst of the English Civil War. Turning in desperation to the Church of Scotland, he wrote, "I beseech you, in the bowels of Christ, think it possible you might be mistaken."[2] Cromwell's cry has been used for everything from the basis of a rule in statistical probability (called "Cromwell's rule") to the ringing end note of Jacob Bronowski's documentary about the genealogy of science, *The Ascent of Man*. Who doesn't want to make those words to live by? Who wants to be on the side of "No, thanks. I'm convinced of the divine right of kings"?

Meanwhile, history's only visible enemies of the slogan "Doubt everything" are much less fun to align yourself with, what with all the burning of books and "heretics" in the name of their own confidence. In 1258 the Mongols' Christian allies were so confident that there had been nothing of worth before Christ that they hurled the contents of the library of Baghdad into the Tigris, reportedly making its waters run black with ink; some servants of the Catholic Church were so confident of the dogma *Ecclesiam nulla salus* (Outside the church, there is no salvation) that they made a saint out of sixteenth-century lawyer Thomas More, who put people on the rack for reading the Bible in English, and in the twenty-first century made a pope of Joseph Ratzinger, who told bishops on pain of excommunication that cases of child abuse were "subject to the pontifical secret."[3] Of course, it's vastly probable that these acts were motivated as much by power as by sincere belief, but even so it's not difficult to feel attracted to the rule "Doubt everything" when certainties seem to leave their bootprints on other people's necks.

The other part of the association between doubt and intellectual bravery, I think, is the fact that it has some powerfully memorable philosophers to its name. René Descartes, sometimes called the father of rationalism, is a special favorite of the canon for his six-part *Meditations*, in which he throws out his old beliefs and decides to "commence to build anew from the foundation" by bringing sight, smell, touch, and so on "in the sphere of doubt."[4] We follow the narrator as he sits fireside in his dressing gown and progressively unpicks his beliefs (I am seated here; these are indeed my hands) by subjecting them to as much doubt as possible (I could be asleep; an evil demon could be deceiving me). His certainties unravel at gathering pace until the only thought he feels able to prove is the famous one: "I think, therefore I am." Descartes notoriously didn't reject God with this same skepticism, at least not out loud, but who could blame him—a few years before the *Meditations* he had written a heliocentric model of the universe called *The World*, but when he heard from a bookseller what had happened to Galileo, he got spooked and nearly burned all his papers. He wrote to a friend, "I have decided to suppress the treatise, and to forfeit almost all my work of the last four years in order to give my obedience to the Church." I remember feeling in my first philosophy classes that there was something deeply moving about inheriting Descartes's mission of doubt, knowing that we could safely take his method where he could not.

And I remember nearly roaring in affirmation when they taught us about William Clifford, who is about as far from Descartes's foppish fireside pontificator as it's possible to be, but just as devoted to doubt. Clifford was a nineteenth-century English mathematician, vast and bearded, who nearly drowned in a shipwreck off the coast of Sicily on his way to see an eclipse when he was twenty-five years old. For totally unrelated reasons, he then wrote a treatise called "The Ethics of Belief," which begins with an "imagined" shipowner wondering to himself whether his ship is seaworthy, but ultimately dismissing his suspicions about the contractors who built his vessel. "In such ways he acquired a sincere and comfortable conviction that his vessel was thoroughly safe and seaworthy; he watched her departure with a light heart... and he got his insurance-money when she went down in mid-ocean and told no tales." What are we to make of the shipowner? "He had no right to believe on such evidence as was before him," says Clifford, and the fact that he did not doubt more is presented not just as a *rational* failing but as a *moral* one. This is Clifford's big move: the explicit connection between doubt and moral courage. "If a man...keeps down and pushes away any doubts which arise about [his beliefs] in his mind—the life of that man is one long sin against mankind."[5]

I loved the pure anarchy of the way philosophy like this tried to leave you with less knowledge instead of more. I loved that you were permitted—encouraged—to doubt things, that you could walk into a class about human rights and leave doubting what a "human" even was, or that you were allowed to think an infinite regress of "Who says?" was profound instead of adolescent. Now, when I ask students why they've chosen philosophy, they often answer in a similar vein. They are here to question what they know, they'll say, in a way that makes it clear that this sort of doubt is an exercise in character as well as enlightenment. They know that rationality means chasing doubt.

"And did you feel certain of John, and safe?" I ask Susie.

"Yes," she says. "Yes."

Susie and John had opted for a traditional wedding ceremony, complete with the bit about "for better and for worse," but about seven years into their marriage, "worse" was in the lead. Raising a young child was expensive; John developed an eye problem that made it difficult for him to see, with treatments that were existentially and financially stressful; then a cherished relative died unexpectedly. The glacé cherry on the misery sundae came when John lost his job. "And this was just after 9/11, so not a lot of people were hiring," Susie remembers.

John stayed in the doldrums of continued unemployment for months, searching for unsatisfying work and finding the search unsatisfying. Susie picked up more hospital social work, though it was hard going. "Hospitals, they're not the most flexible of environments," she says, doing the silver-lining laugh. She would come home exhausted at the end of the day and find the household chores undone. "Looking back, I know why, because John was doing a lot of...extra-curricular activities. He was home with our baby, and I was like, 'What the heck does he do all day?' But then how many husbands could you say that about? A lot."

They enlisted the help of a marriage counselor but still reenacted the same fights over and over—"Just get a job at Home Depot!" "It's *beneath* me!" At last some light broke. A recruiter contacted Susie with an offer of a different job. Fewer hours. More money. No question.

"So [to celebrate], we decided to go out on a date. Our daughter was two at that point, so we were getting a babysitter. I had one of those documents that had all our numbers on it for babysitters, and I was looking through the computer going, '*Ugh*, where is it?' It had Grandma's, the pediatrician, all that, and I couldn't find it. Then I find this folder called 'Life logs,' and I think, *Maybe it's in there.* I open the document, and it was a list, a list of names, that had a couple of girlfriends that I knew of before me. Then it had my name, and then it scrolled on a little further, and it started to have some male names in it as well as female names. And next to the names were descriptions of sexual activities that he had done with these people. It was things like 'Blow job on couch in basement' or 'Went to his garage,' like, pretty descriptive and specific things."

Susie's heart unraveled like the chain on a dropped anchor. "The phrase I keep remembering is 'I no longer trusted the ground beneath my feet.' I did not know what was up and what was down, and what was true and what was not true. I remember that very distinctly. That was my *life*, this family that I had built...I also remember that I made the decision to not confront him with it right away, because I realized I just did not know what was going on. I just knew I needed someone with me when I confronted him about this."

Hurrying before John got home, Susie pressed "print," sequestered a copy to bring up at their next counseling session, put on her lipstick, and went on the date. "I faked it. No one would have ever known. How I did that, I have no freakin' clue."

This moment happened years ago, when the "print" button on most computers was a little printer-shaped icon, smaller than the nail on your little finger, and you clicked it with an actual rolling mouse that sat under your hand. It wasn't impossible for a person with shaking hands to accidentally click "print" twice without realizing and then shut down the computer.

The next day, John turned the computer on to the click-whirr noise of the printer reeling out his own forensically recorded list of infidelities. Not since HAL refused to open the pod-bay doors in *2001: A Space Odyssey* has a computer's single move so comprehensively betrayed both of its masters.

"He was like, 'What the hell is this list? What is this—what did you print out?' This was the beginning of him trying to turn things around and trying to make me feel crazy. I said, 'I saw this, I printed it out, and I was going to talk about it with the therapist,' and he goes, 'Well, this must be a virus.'"

Really? A list with my name on it? That's not how viruses work, she thought, and to prove it she took the computer to a data-recovery expert, where the guy behind the desk exhumed the truth from the computer: along with the usual digital detritus like pictures of kids and half-finished work documents, there were the explicit chat logs, the photographs, the evidence of his meetings with ex-girlfriends. Whatever the bill was for the full day's labor, the computer guy didn't charge it. He had just discovered his own girlfriend had engaged in a similar-scale deceit, and he spent the morning commiserating with Susie over the viscera of the autopsied computer. *You think you know somebody, huh?*

Susie withdrew half their savings and told John to leave their house. At first. Over the next four months she still wasn't sure. "I remember thinking I just had to figure out 'What *is* this? Does he have a sex addiction? What *is* it?' I'm not real religious, but I'd made a vow. People get through affairs, right? And we had a family. I wasn't ready to call it quits." John stopped trying to deny it; he told her he was a sex addict, that he was sick with guilt and would do whatever it took to hold on to their marriage. "We were doing therapy; he was doing a [twelve-step] group—he said he was. But things weren't adding up—he would disappear, he would turn off his phone, he would say he was at work, and I would drive there and he wasn't there. Slowly I started realizing: *This isn't true.*"

Moments ago you read that John had pictures of kids on his computer, and because you're encountering this as narrative, that might have seemed like a red flag. But life doesn't feel like a narrative when you're living it, and we don't expect so many loose ends to tie into a neat explanatory bow. Maybe those pictures were from birthday parties; maybe he had tested a new camera by stepping outside while some kids happened to be walking home; maybe one of his mistresses had kids. Who knows why he had ordinary pictures of children on his computer?

The police knew why.

But Susie didn't find out from the police. She found out because John told her.

"About four months after finding that list, I found a bill that proved that he wasn't where he was supposed to be, you know, that he was still having an affair with this one particular ex-girlfriend. I told him, 'Clearly, you're not working on this, and you need to leave.' I got him a hotel room and arranged for him to be comfortable and all that, but at that point he became completely suicidal. I got him into a hospital here, and during that time he confessed."

Susie recounts these moments like someone who has had to repeat them over and over to authorities. It's a sort of clarity unembellished by her own emotions that makes it feel sometimes like she might be the one breaking bad news to *me*, trying not to take up all the conversational space available for distress.

"He wrote me [a] seven-page letter. He admitted that he had first abused a child when he was twelve. He had touched a child—a little girl—when he was babysitting. This is detailed, but it's important for later. He had touched her, and when her parents got home she was pointing at private parts and [that kind of warning sign], and they questioned him, and he just kind of said, 'Nothing happened.' Then this letter went on to admit that he had masturbated in front of kids when he was in high school, and continued it...His target audience was twelve to fourteen. That was his age range."

Susie found the authorities she needed to speak to. She took a photograph of John to their daughter's school so they would know not to let him in. She went straight to a divorce attorney.

"I wanted to tell [John] I was filing for divorce, but my attorney said, 'You can't do that—he might leave.'" The fear was that John, suicidal and knowing he had just confessed to a crime, would simply get in his car and not come back. The hospital had no legal right to stop him from leaving. "So I didn't tell him, but that kind of went against my I'm-going-to-be-open-and-honest strategy. I saw him once when I knew I was filing but he didn't, and after that the only time I let him back in the house was when I let him back in the garage—I packed up all his stuff and put it in the garage, but he was not even allowed in the house. And then I saw him at court appearances, and that was it."

"Were you afraid to have him around your daughter?"

"Yes. Yes. I remember, actually, the social worker at the hospital— and this was definitely a professional courtesy, because she should not have told me this stuff—she pulled me aside and she said, 'You need to not have him come home.' She said, 'He shows more affection for your dog than he does for you and his daughter. There's something wrong.'"

After their divorce was finalized, Susie heard through a mutual friend that John had been arrested when a child he had groomed online and arranged to meet in person turned out to be a police officer. "He got arrested, and he ended up being charged with sex offenses, ended up on the sex offender registry, and he went to prison for a short amount of time, like very short. But that was all happening during the divorce, [and] I did not realize until later because it happened in another county. While he was in prison I petitioned to have my daughter's name changed to my name, and we went back to my maiden name."

"Does she know what happened?"

"She does, because I had to have talks with her, like, 'Your dad isn't safe' and 'If someone comes up to you and says something...' I told her very age-appropriate things, as we went on. I've been very careful. I don't believe pedophilia is genetic—I believe something happened to John [in his childhood] and I was able to break the cycle because he didn't hurt my daughter. But...I don't want her to think there is this part of her that's bad. So we've been very open about that. I think...this is just guesswork, but I think there was something really wrong in his family. His dad was arrested later for soliciting sex from a minor."

And then there was John's mother. When Susie decided to file for divorce, she felt she owed her mother-in-law an explanation, so she called her. Susie hadn't even mentioned what was in John's seven-page confession letter when his mother interrupted and said, "It's the babysitting thing, isn't it?"

"So she knew," says Susie. "She knew."

Why hadn't Susie? Once she knew John lied, why did she trust him when he said, "I'm just having affairs"? Why didn't she ask what he'd been doing? Why didn't she demand to know who the children in the pictures on John's computer were? Why hadn't she done what William Clifford demanded of us all and *doubted*?

Writer Deborah Schurman-Kauflin argued along these lines in a 2012 article for *Psychology Today* about women whose partners were found to be sexual predators: "Amazingly, these women who were teachers, physician assistants, and charity fundraisers became stunningly stupid when it came to the sex abuse....If for some reason, the wives' pathetic excuse of ignorance doesn't fly, the women immediately run for the sympathy card."[6] Schurman-Kauflin's work may be fringe—her website regretfully announces that she simply no longer has time for pro bono psychic readings—but her view here isn't.

When an FBI investigation in 2015 found that former Subway spokesman Jared Fogle had solicited sex with minors, interviewers asked his wife to answer to the masses, wondering, "How could she possibly *not* have known?" When Channel 4 ran a documentary titled *Married to a Paedophile*, documenting the experiences of women in Susie's position, a popular mommy blog was filled with comments by "disgusted" viewers, saying, "They must have known." And in 2016, when the Australian press revealed that a prominent Sydney dance teacher had abused his students, I heard dozens of people who had never met his wife say censorious things about her from underneath a single raised brow. Elsewhere on *Psychology Today*, which has more than 7 million followers on Facebook, articles from other PhD-wielding researchers echo this sentiment with the kind of certainty that makes doubt look good. Psychologist and author Seth Meyers, who has appeared on CNN, Reuters TV, and *Good Morning America* offering clinical insights into high-profile trials, wrote one such article titled "The Wives of Pedophiles Often Know the Truth," in which he claimed that partners "don't focus on the feelings of the victim, because all their energy goes into feeling sorry for themselves because they made a mistake in choosing the wrong man to marry." "Though I don't wish psychological problems on anyone," he wrote, pulling back the sentential slingshot, "the wives of pedophiles should be accountable for having suspicions but dismissing them to protect their husbands or the status quo."[7] (Meyers later apologized.)

The "You should have doubted" censure holds for different sorts of discovery, too. When Sue Klebold's son Dylan and his friend Eric killed thirteen people at Columbine High School in 1999, thousands of strangers sent her letters or stopped her in the supermarket to say she should have seen it coming. One *New York Times* reader responded to a review of her memoir by saying, "Save yourself some money.... Ms. Klebold has nothing to offer any conscientious, loving parent who can spot self-serving rationalization at even a small distance."[8]

Perhaps you don't want to react like this. But if you subscribe to the "Doubt everything" school of rationality, you don't have much choice. Intellectual bravery requires regularly subjecting our most beloved beliefs to a caustic evidence scrub down. Clifford pulls no punches on this point: "If the belief has been accepted on insufficient evidence, the pleasure is a stolen one.... [I]t is sinful, because it is stolen in defiance of our duty to mankind.... The credulous man is father to the liar and the cheat."

"Was there a moment where you felt ashamed, or implicated in some way?" I ask Susie.

"Yes. I felt like I was conscious of—I still am, to this day—conscious of how I was judged for not knowing, for not realizing. I just used to never tell people until I was sure they wouldn't judge me."

When other people ask "How could you not have known?" with this much frequency and venom, it's not surprising that we ask it of ourselves in the same accusatory tones, seeing in our failure to doubt a fundamental failure to be reasonable. Few of us have been in positions like Susie's. But most of us know what it is to feel ashamed after a discovery and to ask *How could I not have known?* and mentally smacking ourselves in the forehead with an open palm for the exact sort of self-serving, fiction-sustaining doubtlessness that we hate to see in other people. It happens even in low-grade betrayals, like when we take a close friend's assurances that they're good for the money or believe someone we walked away from when they swear that this time it's different.

But all this shame at the altar of truth is of no interest to truth itself. What if, in its fervor for keeping people in touch with the truth, the "Doubt everything" rule in fact drives us further from it, doubles the awful realizations we must accept in these moments, one for the discovery itself, and one for the associated realization that we were foolish enough to miss it? What if doubling the horror of conclusion gives us twice the reasons to push it away?

Dottie Sandusky, wife of former Penn State football coach Jerry Sandusky, has spent years apparently sincerely believing that her husband is innocent of all forty-five counts of sexual abuse for which he is currently imprisoned. Her son has said that during the years Dottie lived with Jerry in their cottage with the spongy lawn, Dottie walked in on things that "most wives would think to be inappropriate,"[9] but over years of trials she has insisted her husband's accusers are wrong or "saw money." At this stage she is apparently unable to entertain the concept of being in denial long enough to say she isn't—in 2014 she was interviewed by Matt Lauer of the *Today* show (before he, in turn, was fired for sexual misconduct),[10] and when he asked whether she "had any doubts," she was confused and asked him to explain the question. When he asked whether she had "let herself consider" whether she "might have blocked something out," she looked at him as though this was about as sensible as asking whether she'd ever considered knitting with jelly.

"No!" she exclaimed.

"But Mrs. Sandusky," Lauer said, "a lot of people say, 'If she's not lying, she's living in denial.'"

"I'm not a lying person," she replied, apparently unaware of the conclusion her answer implies.

This, not Clifford's unchecked orthodoxies, is what strikes me as most dangerous. We have sophisticated and labyrinthine ways of resisting evidence when it asks us to accept conclusions we cannot bear. We splinter ourselves; we splinter our minds. It is as though the force of some discoveries assaults the mind instead of the belief itself, so that the previously cogent mind is the one that buckles, like a winded rower on the end of a jammed oar. In a way it makes a twisted sort of sense: if the self is impugned by the consequences of reason, divest the self of reason.

Often when I discussed Susie's case with people, they would say something like, "Did she really change her mind? It's not like she had a choice." It's tempting to think that the only possible response to evidence this size is to look straight at it. But to think that ignores what most of us know from our own lives or from trying to make the people we love see what's right in front of them: we can take steps back from reality in order to avoid the things we fear will shame us. *Sho doesn't love you. Your daughter is anorexic. Your relationship is abusive. How could you not have known?*

If you have ever tried to talk someone into seeing something that they are ashamed of, you will know that getting people to reckon with these facts is one of the most difficult persuasive tasks it's possible to face. At least the atrophied views Clifford despises might still be responsive to evidence once we eventually get around to interrogating them. But the twisted ironwork we make in our own heads to avoid certain conclusions is far less amenable to the usual mechanisms of persuasion. If we are at all serious about persuasion, we should want to know how to keep minds open to conclusions that might impugn them; we need to know how to stop the specter of shame making people retreat from the evidence at the times they need it most. What if it turns out that the source of all this shame, the idea that we "should have doubted more," is itself worth doubting?

Doubting and rigorously investigating propositions requires rigorously investigating the people who make them. But how inappropriate, paranoid, and suspicious do we think partners or friends are when they put each of our statements through an evidential wringer? Don't we feel violated or besmirched when our loved ones fact-check our stories, calling around to see if we were wherever we said we were?

Think about skepticism personified, and what do you see? I'm not at all sure you see the face of intellectual bravery. I think you see someone incapable of ordinary intimacy, vacillating between paranoia and contempt. You see someone who has despaired of loving connection and who has fled from the possibility of being humiliated again by retreating into pseudo-stoic isolation. In 1896 William James described this sort of person, in response to Clifford's invective, as "one who would shut himself up in snarling logicality...[a man who] would cut himself off by such churlishness from all the social rewards that a more trusting spirit would earn."[11]

My friend Dan Dixon is a literary theorist and writer in Sydney who spent his dissertation years investigating what it is to have a "relationship" with an author. He likes to draw a parallel between the suspension of disbelief in fiction and the suspension of disbelief in relationships. He says, I think rightly, that it's odd to speak of the "willing" suspension of disbelief as though it is an effortful process, when in fact it's a kind of frictionless delight. Nobody settles into the setup of a film or the early stages of a romance and has to remind themselves to turn their skepticism off. Even the sort of person who thinks Descartes was right about everything gets home at the end of the day, hangs up his skepticism, and asks his mother how her day was. It just happens; it's what we do, when we want to be close to something. Sweeping and unrelenting doubt is not the mode we use when we are dealing with the things we love.

This is why proper, rigorous skepticism of our loved ones can be tragically ruinous for those who become ensnared in it. Shakespeare's Othello, mad with doubt about whether his wife, Desdemona, is being unfaithful, falls into fits of rage, actual medical fits, and eventually smothers her with a pillow. He does not recover from his doubt—for that matter, neither does she.

In fact, it's kind of a remarkable grift that skepticism has branded itself as the Move of the Terribly Brave when, in personal settings at least, it is the perfect strategy for avoiding vulnerability. Philosopher Annette Baier, who spent many years working on the nature of care and trust, and their distinctive role in ethics, noted that trust necessarily leaves us open to betrayal.[12] This is what distinguishes trust from mere reliance (nobody is *betrayed* by an alarm clock's failure to do what it said it would). What could be less brave than retreating altogether from the risk of betrayal?

Doubt looks less like an exciting revolutionary here and more like a rationalist Scrooge, padding quietly away to some corner of his lonely castle to polish up his collection of doubts while every chance for the easy trust of friendship or love passes him by.

There are a variety of ways to parse all this so that it opposes Clifford's idea of our "duty" to doubt.

One way is to say that we owe it to each other to be trusting, since so much of our ability to function as intimate, connected, societally embedded creatures depends on it. This inevitably exposes us to certain risks, to be sure, but as Welsh philosopher D. O. Thomas put it, "[It is an error] to exalt this reason into an over-riding one. The safest policy for all to adopt may be one that does not allow every member to do what [is] safest for him."[13]

Another is to say that trust has its own claim to being rational, since placing our trust in people can be precisely what encourages them to live up to it. Princeton philosopher Tori McGeer has argued that in such cases, "trusting beyond evidence can be a robustly rational thing to do."[14]

Whatever the rational status of trust, to feel ashamed that we did not sufficiently doubt those closest to us misses the necessity—the pleasure, even—of suspending doubt.

For a long time Susie wondered whether she had done something wrong by not doubting more of John's story. She imagined what people were saying or thinking about her; John himself voiced what she was afraid to hear.

"One of the things he told me—he really tried to turn this around on me—was that I made it easy for him to lie to me. He said he would tell me a partial story and that I made it easy for him to lie to me."

But once she heard it out loud, she realized this—just like everything else—was not something she should take John's word for.

"I remember thinking, *Yeah, because that's what you do when you trust people.* That's what you do. Otherwise, you'd be interrogating everyone that you were with all the time. I just loved and trusted the wrong person.

"I think that, for me, there wasn't *that* much to see. I could go back with what I know now and say, 'So, that's where he was then,' but I didn't have that information *at the time*. And that's one of the phrases I use for parents for decisions about kids' treatments—you make the best decision that you [can] at the time, and you use the information that you have. And you try your hardest not to look backwards. That's really hard, but you try."

Not long after his arrest, John passed away. "Which honestly, I know it sounds bad, but it was a blessing.

"Nowadays I feel like people really can't know me until they know this story. So it's changed from 'I won't tell you until I can be sure I can trust you' to 'The only way I can be sure you know me is if you know this story.'"

"Do you think that corresponds to you feeling like it's okay that you didn't know?" I want to know.

"Maybe. Maybe. And time, and integrating it into—that it is a part of me, and it doesn't make me a bad person. I've done a lot of thinking about what it means to be bruised, what it means to be broken, and—have you seen the Japanese pottery that's broken but it's filled with gold? That's what I like to think I am. I'm not an athlete. I'm an overweight, middle-aged mom, but six years after I did a hundred-mile bike ride. It was a leukemia fund-raiser, so I did it partly in honor of a lot of my patients, but I really did it to prove I wasn't broken. To prove that he hadn't broken me."

"And you did it."

"I did it. And then I gained all the weight back!"

Susie spent a long time trying to find rational strategies to avoid being hoodwinked. She stopped trusting other people; she stopped trusting herself. For years she could not even think about the possibility of a romantic relationship, and the circle of people she felt comfortable with shrank to her immediate family and her therapist. But more than a decade after her discovery, Susie has found a new romantic relationship and finds herself facing the philosophical question I've been asking: When intimacy requires risk, is it rational to avoid either?

"It's strange actually—his wife left him after twenty-five years, so he has some similar but not matching baggage, that thing of 'I thought everything was okay, but it wasn't.' I said to him, 'You just need to realize there's some stuff he's done to my head that you're going to be stuck with.' And he's like, 'That's okay. I'm okay with that.'"

When Susie told her daughter about her new relationship, she was prepared for her daughter to be resistant to the idea.

"But this just came out of her wonderful mouth the other day. She said, 'You know what, Mom? I know a lot of stuff happened with my dad, but I think this is worth it. Nothing could be as bad as what my dad did. It's worth it, even if you risk getting your heart broken again.'"

And that, at least, Susie did not doubt.

chapter five

Learning to Forget What You Never Really Knew

People almost invariably arrive
at their beliefs not on the basis
of proof but on the basis of
what they find attractive.
—BLAISE PASCAL

Monsieur Pascal has too much
vacuum in his brain.
—RENÉ DESCARTES

Here's a plausible-sounding rule: change your mind when, and only when, there is more evidence for one side than the other. If the evidence does not resolve things, suspend judgment.

If that's right, then it's very strange that Nicole changes her mind as often as she does. All the evidence is fixed and unchanging, sealed on videotapes and in evidence files in the courts. But Nicole, experts in psychology, and hundreds of people interested in her case are still divided over what really happened.

There are two parts to the story: what happened to Nicole when she was not yet seven and what happened when she was seventeen. The first part begins when Nicole's parents' marriage soured into a bitter custody battle and it was alleged that Nicole had been abused by her mother. Nicole's mother denied it, and the family court sent David Corwin to break the impasse.

Dr. David Corwin is a forensic and child psychiatrist specializing in child abuse. He chaired the group that founded the American Professional Society on the Abuse of Children, and by the time he was called to Nicole's case he had already interviewed dozens of children in similar situations. Corwin was to conduct a series of interviews with Nicole and her family and then make a custody recommendation to the court. In the transcripts from those interviews,[1] Nicole says her mother has hurt her in the bathtub; her mother has burned her feet.

> CORWIN: [Nicole], listen closely, did those things actually happen?
> NICOLE: Yes.
> CORWIN: Is that the truth?
> NICOLE: Yes.

There were other troubling signs. Nicole seemed nervous when her mother sat outside Corwin's office and asked him anxiously whether his microphone could "talk" to the waiting area where her mother sat. On separate occasions, Corwin asked each of Nicole's parents to join their daughter in the interview room and asked them each to instruct Nicole to tell the truth. Corwin paid close attention to how they reacted. "Just tell the truth, that's what the doctor wants to hear," said her father. But when it was Nicole's mother's turn, she said, "Do you remember what we talked about? What'd you tell Mommy?"

"No," Corwin steers, "what I want you to tell her is to tell me the truth."

Days later Nicole appeared in an emergency room with her mother and grandmother, this time saying that her father had abused her. But the next day, Nicole told a social worker she had made up the story because her mother had threatened to hit her if she didn't.

Corwin scheduled one more last-minute interview with Nicole, the same day he was due to testify in court, to ask what had happened:

> NICOLE: [Mom] threatened me that if I didn't lie to the CPS that she would do something bad to me.
> CORWIN: Are you a Girl Scout or a Brownie or anything like that?
> NICOLE: I'm a Brownie.
> CORWIN: Okay. So what you just told me, do you promise on your oath as a Brownie, do you promise God that you're telling the truth?
> NICOLE: (Nods yes).

Nicole's mother lost custody and was not allowed visitation rights.

For ten years, that was that. But then there's the second part of the story, the part that happened when Nicole was sixteen. I spoke to Dr. Corwin from his office in Utah, where he still works in child forensic psychiatry and pediatric trauma, and asked him what he remembered of the events that came next. From pictures you might be tempted to compare him to Colonel Sanders if the colonel had become a doctor instead of going into fried chicken—he has a high forehead, a white mustache, and a puffy halo of white-gray hair—but the comparison only sticks in pictures because when Corwin speaks, he's no jovial cartoon character. He is sober, precise, and a little guarded with me, but it turns out the answer to the question about what he remembers is "a lot."

"I called [Nicole's] father because I was being asked to speak to the American Academy of Pediatrics [on the topic] 'Should we believe what children tell us about child abuse?' I had thirteen minutes to address that topic—in front of four thousand pediatricians. And Nicole's video was one of the most compelling descriptions of abuse I had seen in my professional experience. So I was seeking her father's consent, and her assent, to show it in a big forum. I had sought their permission several years earlier to show it under controlled conditions to a subcommittee of the California Legislature. Her father and she had given me permission before, [but] it had been several years, and I felt that ethically I had a responsibility to make sure that they were still okay with it being used in forums of that type."

Corwin tried to reach Nicole's father via the old means, but discovered that since they'd last spoken, he had had a stroke and Nicole had been moved into foster care.

"I ended up locating him in a convalescent home.... He said yes, that he would confirm his consent, and I said, 'Well, I'd like to speak to Nicole, too.' He gave me the number of the foster home. When I rang, I explained to her why I was calling, and said, 'Is it still okay with you if I show that for professional training?' And she said, 'Sure, Dr. Corwin, anything to help'—that was roughly what she said. So I'm feeling like I've done my ethical duty and was going to wish her well, and there's this little pause and she says, 'But you know something? I can't remember what happened when I was little. Would you please send me the videos?'"

Many reports of this moment have suggested that Nicole had wholesale forgotten alleging the abuse at all. That isn't right, at least not going by the transcripts and her own recollections. She had forgotten the precise claims she'd made, and, more important, she'd forgotten whether they were true. Sometimes she had vivid flashbacks to being held over a stove, but sometimes she had that foggy feeling we get when we can't tell which memories are real and which we've stitched together out of fragmented anecdotes.

She had been worrying about it before Corwin phoned. After her father's stroke, Nicole had reached out to her mother, and they had just started speaking again for the first time since the divorce. She had hoped after her father's stroke that some familial contact would help with her sudden sense of being adrift and alone. It did. With her foster mother's encouragement, she started speaking to her mother more regularly. But it wasn't long before her mother started saying to Nicole what she'd said to Corwin all those years ago: that the abuse story was a lie, that she had never hurt her daughter.

"What if I just said it?" Nicole started wondering aloud to her foster mother. "What if Dad put me up to it?"

When Corwin phoned, Nicole saw a chance to get the evidence that would help her make up her mind. He could just send her the tapes.

Corwin hesitated. He wasn't sure how to respond. "To my knowledge that had never been done, never been studied," he told me. "We had no idea what the possible pluses and minuses are of a young woman looking at such material. I had two thoughts. One was [that] she has a right to know what happened in her life, and on the other hand I thought, 'I certainly don't want that to hurt her, or be upsetting to her.' So I said to her, 'I think it's your right [to see them], but can you wait until I can be there and I can do everything I can to make it a positive experience?'"

About a year later, Corwin happened to be near Nicole's hometown. Nicole's father had died in the intervening time, so Corwin had to locate Nicole through her school, and when he did she told him yes, she still wanted to see the tapes. Corwin arranged to show them to her in the company of her foster mother and a local therapist and with a video camera to record her informed consent.

NICOLE: Do you want little things, or—
CORWIN: Everything. Everything you can remember.
NICOLE: Okay. I remember visually, I remember wooden, like the walls, it was like a wooden paneling, and I remember in one of the interviews I wore a shirt that was striped this way....I remember I was answering questions, and I told you, I guess, I told the court, that my mom abused me, that she burned my feet on a stove,

that's really the most serious accusation against her that I remember, I don't know what else I said.

CORWIN: Okay. Do you remember anything about the concerns about possible sexual abuse?

NICOLE: No, I mean, I remember that was part of the accusation but I don't remember anything else—wait a minute, yeah I do.

CORWIN: What do you remember?

NICOLE: Oh my gosh, that's really really weird. I accused her of taking pictures of me and my brother and selling them and I accused her of—when she was bathing me or whatever, hurting me, and that's—

CORWIN: As you're saying that to me, you remember having said those things or you remember having experienced those things?

NICOLE: I remember saying about the pictures, I remember it happening, that she hurt me.

Nicole went on to repeat several times that she remembered her mother inserting her finger into her vagina while bathing her. It's not clear where the story about the photographs comes from; that wasn't on the original tapes. But her description of the bathtub incident matches what she said as a child, and broadly speaking so does the story about the burns. It seemed to many in the room that Nicole's memory had just given her the certainty she'd been looking for. Corwin played the tapes for her anyway, and when they were finished

Nicole's foster mother said, "I think this has been a beautiful closure." Nicole said now she had a firm belief about what had happened in her childhood. She was sure her mother had abused her. And she seems to prefer that to uncertainty:

CORWIN: Despite its painfulness, do you think that this has been a constructive experience at this point in time?

NICOLE: Yes. There's some questions that might never be answered, you know, I can live with that. My biggest question has been answered. I think it's a very healthy thing not to run from something, just the fact that I turned around and I faced it, that's strength enough to go on, to put it to bed. And next you're going to ask if you can use this for educational purposes, right? Yes, you can.

With Nicole's permission, Corwin began work on a journal article about the incident, calling Nicole "Jane Doe" throughout. Nicole went back to her final years at school, believing that at last she had the evidence to avoid being uncertain.

Withholding belief has something of a brand reputation for being rationally responsible. Agnosticism in the face of indecisive evidence seems like the mature response, one that does justice to the complexity of the situation. As Clarence Darrow famously wrote, "Any one who thinks is an agnostic about something, otherwise he must believe that he is possessed of all knowledge. And the proper place for such a person is in the madhouse or the home for the feeble-minded."[2]

The inverse is true, too; often when we see people leaping to form beliefs when the evidence is indecisive—like when people construe scant evidence from a crush as proof positive that their feelings are reciprocated—we can feel a kind of pity, or a vicarious shame. You should resist such shoddy conclusions when the evidence is indeterminate; you should keep your mind in a kind of suspended animation, floating above all the available hypotheses.

One path to this conclusion, based on a plausible view, goes like this: evidence, and *only* evidence, determines what we should believe. Change your mind when there is enough evidence, but *only* when there is enough. In cases where the evidence on both sides of the belief scale compels it to stay level, suspend judgment, since the only thing that could resolve such an impasse would be more evidence. Considerations like what would be good for us to believe ought not to be able to leap onto the scale and tilt it in either direction. Such considerations are not useful, and they just get muddy paw prints all over the instruments. David Hume's formulation is one of the cleanest—"A wise man ... proportions his belief to the evidence"—and our friend William Clifford's is one of the most fiery: "It is wrong always, everywhere, and for anyone to believe anything on insufficient evidence."[3]

The question about whether other considerations should be allowed to pull us out of agnosticism either is then answered with a resounding no or just dissolves.

Seventeenth-century mathematician and philosopher Blaise Pascal gave us a famously unpersuasive example of a rival thought. *"Au contraire,"* said Pascal (I'm summarizing for efficiency but keeping the authentic French feel). Pragmatic considerations *can* break us out of agnosticism, he suggested, and in at least one case they should. That case has been dubbed "Pascal's wager," and it was the Catholic Pascal's effort to turn agnostics into believers.[4] Suppose God doesn't exist: What harm does it do you to believe he does? Not a great deal—an error, but a harmless one, and you're worm food by the time you discover it. But suppose God *does* exist: What harm does it do you to believe he doesn't? Hell, wrath, posthumous pitchforks. "If you gain, you gain all; if you lose, you lose nothing," wrote Pascal. "Wager, then, without hesitation that He is."

I know of no religious person persuaded by Pascal's wager, not even Pascal himself. Part of his own conversion involved a midnight vision in 1654, long before he wrote the wager, which he saw so vividly he immediately wrote every detail on a small slip of paper, and for the rest of his life he carefully stitched that piece of paper into the lining of his coat, unpicking it and transferring it every time he changed coats. That doesn't look like someone weighing the pragmatic considerations to me; it looks like someone who thinks they have seen an anvil crash down on one side of the evidence scale.

And so reasonably enough, many of us take it for granted that a theory of justified belief has jumped the tracks if it winds up endorsing anything like Pascal's view. Reasons like Pascal's are not what any of us think of when we think of having reasons for a conclusion. Instead, in cases where the evidence seems to recommend agnosticism, we prefer to suspend belief. After all, we can do real damage to real people if we don't.

Just ask Elizabeth Loftus.

Elizabeth Loftus is a psychologist and professor at the University of California, Irvine, who has spent most of her career working on the fallibility of memory and the costs of getting it wrong. When she was a graduate student, she found that people could be induced to "remember" false features of a filmed car accident if they were asked "How fast was the car going when the accident smashed its headlight?" instead of "Did you see any broken glass?" As a professor, she led the famous "Lost in the Mall" experiments, in which experimenters told participants a series of stories that they said were true, like "Your parents told us about the time you got lost in the mall." Participants would "remember" these events and even embellish them with "recollected" details—even if the story was entirely false.

For most of her career, Loftus has worried what damage might be wreaked on the basis of false memories that felt true to the people who held them. In the 1980s came a particularly vivid answer: it emerged that a number of therapists in the UK, Australia, the United States, and Canada had been using hypnosis and strong barbiturates to help their clients pull memories of trauma from their subconscious hiding places, trading on the thought that many adult neuroses were expressions of otherwise completely forgotten trauma. Stories of cartoonish evil, like "Mom and Dad ate the pizza boy," started being recovered as genuine memories, accepted as fact, and used to send people to jail. Loftus's research helped vindicate the flabbergasted accused by proving that the evidence for these memories was as hard to find as the memories themselves had been. Around the world, sentences were overturned and multimillion-dollar settlements reached as clients and therapists had to reckon with the idea that the trauma they had imagined was the root of their problems was just that: imagined. One woman who recovered the memory that her family were cannibals carefully collected a sample from a family lunch, only to have the laboratory send back its nonplussed reply: just beef. By the time David Corwin and his coauthor, Erna Olafson, published an article titled "Videotaped Discovery of a Reportedly Unrecallable Memory of Child Sexual Abuse" in 1997,[5] describing Nicole's experience using the pseudonym "Jane Doe," Loftus had already written the book on the myth of repressed memory. It's called *The Myth of Repressed Memory*.

Loftus read the article about Nicole's sudden recollection and wanted to investigate Nicole's case for herself; she thought it sounded fishy. But the name "Jane Doe" wasn't much to go on, and all the other details that could have identified Nicole were obscured: Nicole's parents lived in "Mumtown" and "Dadtown," the date of her father's death had been changed, and her foster mother was not referred to by her name. Nicole had been a minor at the time of her sudden recollection, and it had been important to Corwin and Olafson to protect her identity.

Loftus broke through that pseudonym.

She spoke to me about the case one evening as she sat in her living room waiting for dinner guests. You have to talk fast with Loftus: she is busy, and you don't scare her. Once, she got a series of death threats for her work on recovered memories; not everyone was delighted to have been proved wrong. So she learned to shoot a gun, and the target practice sheets are still hanging in her office.

"How did you find Nicole's real name?" I ask.

"The very first clue that I got was that one of the people that Corwin sent the tapes to—because they wrote a commentary in the original article—was a former student of mine, who showed me the tapes in my living room. I heard Corwin call her 'Nicole.' Then I heard the name of her real hometown. Those were my first clues. She said her father had died eleven months ago. Then I found a court case with some similar facts. Then I taught myself how to search Social Security records, to plug into the death records. Then I thought, 'I know, I'll write to the newspapers and see if I can get the obituaries, see if anyone left a daughter named Nicole.' It was a long process."

When Loftus had the name of the Jane Doe in the case, she sent a private investigator to Nicole's hometown. Nicole found out that someone had discovered her identity when a friend paged her to ask her why private investigators were knocking on doors.

Here is what Loftus and her team found.

A friend of the family told Loftus's team, "No way did any of the allegations occur." Nicole's mother wept when she heard Loftus thought she might be innocent, saying, "I never thought this day would come." Loftus found concerns about how credible Nicole's father's testimony could have been: she heard that he had drinking problems, and Nicole's grandmother had written to the court to say he had once beaten his own son so that "his entire face was swollen to a pulp and he was unable to move."

Loftus spoke to the woman who had been dating Nicole's father at the time of the allegations. Loftus said that she'd talked about trying to get Nicole away from her mother with what she called "the sexual angle" and said they were "going for broke." Even the burns themselves were open to doubt: Loftus found a letter from another psychologist, saying,

"It was never determined if her feet and hand were indeed burned, since [Nicole] has a fungus condition that causes her skin to blister and peel." Nicole's mother has the same condition—she showed Loftus patches on her fingers where the skin was shedding and sloughing off. Then, the piece of evidence Loftus calls "most impressive": she found reports by another therapist who had investigated the case before Corwin, who had said that Nicole sounded "not spontaneous" and "mechanical and rehearsed" when she talked about abuse.

When Nicole heard someone was looking into her life, she suspected it had to do with Corwin's article. It was the only thing she could think of that would interest an investigator. She phoned Corwin, distressed, and Corwin discovered that Loftus was behind the investigation. Nicole complained to Loftus's university.

"[University staff] basically came to my office and took my files," says Loftus. "I mean, I really couldn't believe this, because I was pretty convinced that I had a case of somebody who was probably falsely accused—I was interested in another human being, and I was going to get in trouble for it? It was shocking. I didn't publish the exposé until [two years later], when I got my neck out of the guillotine."

Loftus and coauthor Melvin Guyer wrote these findings in a two-part article for the *Skeptical Inquirer* titled "Who Abused Jane Doe?"[6] Part 1 concluded, "We believe that there are ample reasons to doubt whether Jane Doe was physically or sexually abused by her mother, and to doubt much of the 'supporting evidence' used to support the abuse hypothesis."

Surrounded as we are by the sorts of stories that Loftus's career has focused on, it's not hard to see why people wind up thinking that rationality favors withholding belief in cases of evidentiary dead heats. Errors have costs. Better to suspend belief and have the guarantee that we have not made a costly mistake. Better, as Loftus puts it, to "doubt the hypothesis" than to risk prematurely believing something that turns out to be wrong.

But notice that if we take this line of thought, we're no longer considering evidence and only evidence. The question has stopped being about whether the evidence has anointed a particular hypothesis the right one and started being about whether there are *other* good reasons for refusing to hold either hypothesis—good reasons like the cost we would have to answer for if we believed it, and it turned out to be wrong.

But it's worth noticing, as William James did, that "believing truth" and "shunning error" turn out to be two materially different missions, with opposing recommendations about what to do when the evidence is indecisive.[7] "We may regard the chase for truth as paramount, and the avoidance of error as secondary," James explains, "or we may, on the other hand, treat the avoidance of error as more imperative, and let truth take its chance."

So which should we choose?

"What would *you* believe, if you were Nicole?" I ask Loftus.

"Well...I don't know what her relationship with her biological mother is now—if she has a relationship with the biological mother, that would be a pull maybe to not believe it, but if she has a relationship with some of the repression aficionados who might want to keep her believing, they may be an influence. I just don't know. It would be interesting to know. People would wonder, 'Where is [Nicole] today? What is she thinking today?'"

Nicole told me the answer. "Some days I believe it happened, and other days I don't. I still go back and forth. The majority of days I just accept that it happened, but...there are still days when I don't believe it."

Nicole is a grown woman now. She's married; she has a rottweiler; she rides motorbikes. I realized just before I spoke to her that I had no idea what sort of person she might be. So much of the material you read about her lets her actual character recede into folds of plot points. First she is literally nameless, a "Jane Doe" you aren't meant to be able to picture. Then she is pushed and pulled through child protection systems where lawyers and psychiatrists and foster workers speak on her behalf because legally she can't do it alone. When she finally acts under her own name and volition by complaining to Loftus's university, it is because hundreds of people have become interested in a story where she features mainly as a mute figure. She is the person we do not hear from, who facilitates the plot but whom we don't know much about, like a parent killed off in the first chapters of a Roald Dahl book.

But her life is exactly the opposite of this picture—it is firm, self-directed, knowable. She graduated in the top 5 percent of her high school, enlisted with the US Navy when she was eighteen, and became a helicopter pilot, flying pointy-nosed *Apocalypse Now*–looking behemoths with blacked-out windows and scary names like "Seahawk." She was stationed in Hawaii, did routine military-grade fitness tests, and won a navy scholarship to go to college where she earned a BA in psychology. In fact, she got three more degrees in psychology—two master's and a PhD. She now practices in a clinic not far from where she grew up, and she is careful to tell me that what she says in our interview is not professional advice. She has the same mop of tight brunette curls she had as a child and the same wide, almost leonine face. Her cheeks stand out from the rest of her face in high relief, and she has one deep dimple when she smiles, but ours is not a smiling conversation.

"It was surreal to sit there and watch yourself knowing that it's you. It's still surreal, even when I watch those videos now. I had hoped that my whole memory would come back, that I could see the little girl in those tapes and it would be resolved once and for all. That didn't happen. Actually, for a while it did resolve it, for a brief period of time, and then all of the Loftus stuff threw it back into doubt."

Nicole found out about Loftus's article when it was already on newsstands. She and a friend from her naval station went to a bookstore to buy a copy and read it together, shocked. Even though Loftus had reverted to the original "Jane Doe" pseudonym, Nicole sued for defamation and invasion of privacy.

Part of the problem was that when Nicole read the article, she saw errors.

Loftus's article wrongly claimed that Corwin had sought Nicole out with the express purpose of discovering "what, if anything" Nicole had remembered. It wrongly stated that Corwin telephoned Nicole's foster mother, "saying he was doing research and wanted to interview [Nicole] again." It wrongly stated that Corwin believed the incident was proof of repressed memory. Corwin was unambiguous when he spoke to me: "We never claimed that we'd proven this or that," he said. "We just said, 'This is interesting, and it's presented here for discussion.' We didn't take a strong position with regard to what it meant. We did raise the question that there are hundreds of thousands, maybe millions, of these [forensic] videos in existence. What is the duty of the systems that maintain them? What are the rights of the children as they get older to know the basis of what happened during their childhoods? We asked that question. But no one's touched that."

Loftus's article wrongly claimed, as Loftus did in a TED Talk in 2003, that Corwin had been showing the tapes "in public." Corwin does not show them in public, only at professional events. When he presented them at the California Legislature, the TV screens were turned so that the video was not visible from the gallery. And Nicole was angry that she hadn't been consulted more about Loftus's decision to investigate. These arguments shuttled back and forth for years during the lawsuit, each one trailing clouds of footnotes. Years later, mutually exhausted, Loftus and Nicole reached a settlement.

"When the lawyers were trying to negotiate some sort of settlement, they said to me, 'Is there anything that you can apologize for?' The only thing I could think of was that I was sorry that she felt so hurt by this effort, but I wasn't sorry that I stepped in to support what I thought—and now probably believe even more strongly—was a falsely accused woman.... People want to say, 'This is [Nicole's] story, her rights, only her rights.' She's not the only person in this story! How about the option that she realizes that maybe, possibly, [the abuse] didn't happen, that she reunites with her mother, and the mother has a daughter? That might have been a happy ending."

"Was that what you hoped would happen?" I ask.

"I might have even had a little fantasy that that might happen."

Things looked different to Nicole.

"I still haven't found one piece of evidence that sways me one way or the other," she says. Instead, Nicole's mind has changed for years like a weathervane in a hurricane

"When I watch [the videos] it's very difficult to believe that that little girl is lying. So when I think about that, I'm almost unanimously persuaded that it did happen."

"How do you feel about the girl in those tapes on the days when you believe it *didn't* happen?"

"I don't know if I even have an answer to that question. I mean, she believed what she was saying, but I was either coerced or tricked into believing that that was true."

"It's interesting that you talk about those videos in the third person, like 'that girl' and 'that person.' Does it not feel like it's you?"

"At times it doesn't. I think I talk about it more in the third person when I'm talking about it not having happened be-cause it's hard for me to own that part of myself, if I'm be-lieving that I lied or was somehow not truthful in what I was saying."

"What does it do to a person, to have to withhold judg-ment about something this big?"

Nicole is quiet for so long, I think the line might have gone dead.

"That uncertainty...it was the ether that I lived in. It was all around me, all the time. It affected every *single* relation-ship, in every possible way. It requires me to have a sense of self that is not dependent on whether I was sexually assaulted by my mother. It's a really big ask."

In some ways Nicole's story looks like a story about the costs and pragmatic consequences of various beliefs. She told me that those things weigh on her as much as the evidence itself.

"On the days when I believe that it happened, I know that I am *willing* myself to believe that it's true because there are people out there who believe strongly that it happened, and because I don't want Elizabeth Loftus to be right. Going the other way, it takes a little less work, but I know I'm willing myself."

In other ways, though, her story is about more than costs of belief: it is about the costs of withholding, too. If costs of error matter to us, why not the costs of withholding?

Believing something to be false is not the only way to cause monstrous shock waves and incalculable damage. Failing to believe something that turns out to be true can be costly in similar ways, or at least to similar degrees.

Nicole's mother is alive, for instance. Should Nicole speak to her, or not? Suppose her mother is innocent, and, instead of believing that, Nicole spends her life suspending judgment. Are the costs Nicole—and her mother—would have to bear any better than the costs they would bear if she falsely believed "She did it"? I'm not sure they are: the actions of a person uncertain about whether their mother abused them can look very much like the actions of a person who positively believes she did. In neither case will their mother be entirely trusted with the grandkids; in neither case will she be vindicated; in neither case will their relationship be free of the strain of suspicion.

The problem here is that it's difficult to find an action as lukewarm as the mental state of a person who isn't sure what to believe. In the domain of belief, typically we have three options: believe the thing, reject it, or suspend judgment. But as noted by Richard Feldman, a philosopher whose work on rationality is so prolific they gave him his own conference called "Feldmania," when it comes to actions, sometimes we find ourselves down to two options: do the thing, or don't. "Hesitating forever is the same as not doing it," Feldman noted. Speak to your mother, or don't.[8]

Remarkably, Nicole does speak to her mother. She's always wanted to have a relationship with her, right from when she first reached out to her mom while she was in foster care. But it is not an ordinary relationship. It's strained, and sometimes buckles under the weight of what Nicole can't know.

"There was a conversation not too terribly long ago when she said she was going to write out her justification for how I should know that this didn't happen, but I've yet to see that, and I don't even know if I want to. I just don't believe that she could convince me one way or the other."

"Was there ever a time where you just…got on easily?"

"There have been times like that, but rather quickly it seems to come back to…she wants me to be a seven-year-old. She doesn't want me to be a forty-year-old. I'll give you an example: on my thirty-seventh birthday, she threw me a seven-year-old's party," Nicole recalls. "The cake had to have my favorite flowers on it; she sent one of my friends to the store to get ice cream. It was just...I realized in that moment that I could just never give her what she wants from me, to go back in time and be allowed to mother me again. It's...it's a very strained relationship."

If the costs of error matter, why not these costs, too, the costs of withholding belief? Some philosophers have answered simply: "they do."

But one of the weirder consequences of thinking that costs matter, though, is that we will wind up with the verdict that different people facing the same evidence ought to believe different things depending on the stakes and costs around them. Maybe this seems a little skew-whiff to you; maybe you don't like the thought that what it's rational to do could depend on features about a given thinker. Perhaps you're sympathetic to Tyler Burge's thought in his work on justifications for and entitlement to beliefs: "Reason has a function in providing guidance to truth, in presenting and promoting truth without regard to individual interest. That is why [reasons for belief] are not relativized to a person or to a desire."[9]

Whatever the aims of rationality and the status of costs of error, Nicole's story gives us cause to rethink our confidence that reason favors withholding belief in all cases where the evidence is indecisive. It may yet turn out that that view is right, but it will be for far more complex reasons than we have in mind when we act the way I said we do at the start of this story, as we look with a mixture of pity and vicarious shame on people who leap to believe their crush reciprocates their feelings. Even if our reaction turns out to be justified, we will still have important unanswered questions about what rationality aims at and about whether costs matter, and why.

If we're uncertain about uncertainty itself, the better question may be how to bear it. Some beliefs bear more weight than others, like Nicole's pre-Loftus view that she just was, straightforwardly, a victim of childhood abuse. It mattered to her; it held up her sense of self. We each have versions of these beliefs: I have great confidence in my family; you might have great confidence in your God. Finding ourselves suddenly uncertain about these load-bearing things can be disruptively preoccupying, especially when each of the available verdicts threatens the beliefs we least want to surrender. It can calcify into obsession, making us worry at a question like a loose tooth, returning over and over in our vacant moments to the promise of a definitive answer. The cruelty here is that the more urgently we dig into and flail around inside the question, the more central we make that uncertainty in our lives and the higher we drive the costs of having to stay in it. Ask anyone who's wondered whether their partner is lying or which parts of their lifestyle are exacerbating their chronic pain: it is maddening in the literal sense of the word.

If we want people to be able to stay in uncertainty about the things that really matter, the strategy may be less about injunctions to withhold belief and more about making these uncertainties bear a little less weight.

"I have to sort of build my life, my sense of self around being a wife, and a Christian, and a psychologist, and a friend. Those are the parts of my identity I build on," Nicole explains. "It's a matter of making the conscious choice over and over again, until it's a habit, to consider other things and other parts of myself. In a way it's healthy, I think. Some people are able to build on their identities as survivors in a very healthy way, and then some people absolutely are not. When I finally made the choice to start living otherwise, it's just like dieting: you start, and then you lose your motivation and you go back to the way you used to eat. I would start, and then I would revert back to my old way of thinking. All told it probably took several years for me to adjust completely."

"Do you have anything you'd say to people who are having to live with really heavy uncertainty?" I ask.

"That's a really tough one," Nicole answers, after thinking for a while. "It's just like forgiveness, in that everyone has to do it in their own time. If you try to rush someone, they're just going to dig their heels in and say, 'Leave me alone.' Everyone has to make a decision for themselves as to when it's time to move on. I didn't want to get to the end of my life and know that I lived my entire life in fear. I'm not saying it will happen overnight, but . . . it can get easier."

As I researched Nicole's story, over and over, people would ask me, "So *did* it happen?" Uncertainty, whatever its costs, is deeply unsatisfying. But there isn't an answer—or, rather, there is, and we don't know it. All we have is the evidence that both sides say matters most—and the question, as always, of what it's rational to believe.

chapter six

How I Learned to Stop Worrying and Love the Truth Bomb

The feelings of our heart, the
agitation of our passions, the
vehemence of our affections,
dissipate all its conclusions,
and reduce the profound
philosopher to a mere plebeian.
—DAVID HUME

Hume's philosophy, whether
true or false, represents the
bankruptcy of eighteenth-century
reasonableness.
—BERTRAND RUSSELL

P eter was making jam when the women came to the door. There were two of them, one older than the other, and one carried a camera.

"We used to live here," they told him. "Would you mind if we took a picture from across the street?"

"I thought that was strange right away," says Peter, "because why would you not just take the picture? Why would you bother to come in unless you wanted to have contact with the person inside the house?"

The jam-making operation was taking place in a leafy suburb in Sydney in one of those colonial houses built before electricity, where the telephone and lighting cords snake along the pockmarked baseboards and the doors stick in the frames as the wood gestates in the summer heat.

Peter closed the door and walked back into the house, not sure why he felt so shaken.

"There was just something really weird about it," he remembers. A friend who was with him that day told Peter he'd looked "completely ashen-faced" and "more disturbed than if they'd been a burglar."

The women didn't tell him why they'd really come to the door. In the end, he didn't even find out from them.

Peter had grown up as the only child of adoring parents in small-town New South Wales. "I grew up on a farm. My life was postcard-perfect, really. My parents just adored me. Probably too much, now that I look back on it...They had an incredibly secure relationship, so insecurity just didn't figure in my life."

In fact, his childhood was so idyllic, it became an occupational hazard. In his young adulthood Peter moved to Sydney to train at one of those elite, break-you-down-to-build-you-up drama schools renowned for producing talented method actors who turn trauma into onstage magic. Students sat in circles recounting childhood horror stories to fuel their performances. "And I'd sit there and think, 'I can't think of *anything*! This is awful—I'll have to make something up.'"

It wasn't just Peter's parents who treasured him—the love for him radiated out through concentric circles of family, from aunts to uncles to grandparents out to distant relatives once removed. "In a funny sort of way, I was a bit like a shared child. A lot of them used to make me feel a bit special. They used to lavish so much attention on me...It was a bit embarrassing, actually. I would always get more than the other grandchildren and nephews and nieces." This is saying something, because there were thirty-four other grandchildren.

Peter is now a professional set and costume designer, and the best way to describe his demeanor is to say he has exactly the calm precision and delight in small details you might expect in a person who spends a lot of time with beautiful scale models. I am reliably told that his kitchen cupboards are a kind of hushed temple of matching plastic containers, but that's not to say he is one of those Scandi-minimalist types who wears only linen and abhors a curlicue; often his designs are about capturing the sprawl and complexity of a dramatic production without themselves being sprawling or dramatic. This same ability to capture a lot with very little produces a frighteningly flinty wryness when done with language instead of sets: during press for a production Peter had worked on, an interviewer once asked him, "What's your best party trick?" "Not turning up," said Peter. Measure twice, cut once.

There's a similar aesthetic sense to the way he tells the story that explains the women at the door. He's not in a hurry to prove a point with every detail. Sometimes he just gestures toward his experiences with gentle observational interest. "I did used to have this sense that something was missing. I used to have this fantasy that there was another sense people had—along with sight, sound, smell, and all the rest of it—that made their lives easier. But this could have been anything. It could have been that [I'm] gay and didn't know it [at the time]; it could have been the usual teenage ennui. You can think about these questions for years, and when you *do* come up with an answer, you just think, 'Well, am I just writing a book in my head?'"

How I Learned to Stop Worrying

By the time the women arrived on Peter's doorstep, he was a secure middle-aged man with a partner and a fulfilling career. His father had died not long before, and he had moved his mother to a house close by him so he could care for her in her old age. Macular degeneration had claimed her sight, and Peter had arranged for health care workers to help her in the mornings. In the afternoons, he would go to her house, boil the kettle, pick the mail up off the hallway table, and read it to her over a cup of tea.

A few weeks after the women first appeared, Peter did the teatime ritual as usual. He picked up a letter and read the postmark aloud. "It's from the Department of Social Services," he said. "What could they want?"

"Oh," his mother replied. "Well, before you read... Did it ever occur to you that you might have been adopted?"

It's worth taking a moment to get a sense of the scale of the discovery here. Peter had made it to middle age without finding out that he was adopted, which meant that his parents had hidden it from him for close to five decades. And not just his parents. The physics of small-town secrets demand that either everyone knows or no one knows; in Peter's case, *everyone* knew. "In a little country town, you can't be not-pregnant one day and then have a child the next. There was no secret about it. My dad [went] to the meat market one afternoon, and the butcher said, 'How's the missus?' and my dad said, 'Oh, she's great! She's getting a baby tomorrow.'"

"But *you* never knew?" I ask.

"I mean, I don't think any child gets through life without considering whether it's adopted or not, and some people hope they are. But I can't remember a specific instance where it crossed my mind, and because no one had ever said anything..." He trails off.

"I remember once, actually, when [my partner] Stephen was doing the meet-the-family thing, we had lunch with a whole lot of relatives at my grandmother's house, and in the dining room, there were all these family portraits and photographs going back, like, two hundred years." Maybe Stephen thought Peter resembled them, or maybe he was just making a joke about their sheer quantity, but either way he said, "in front of the *entire* family, 'Well, Peter's someone who never needs to worry about whether he's adopted!' So it's not like it was just a no-brainer—that anyone could see I was adopted."

The women who had come knocking at his door were his biological mother and her daughter—Peter's half sister. They had spent years not knowing where he was or how to contact him because for decades the adoption records of New South Wales were legally "sealed," meaning birth parents could not contact or locate the people who had raised their babies. By the late 1990s, the time we met Peter making jam, advocacy groups had successfully appealed to the government to open the records, allowing people like Peter's birth family to make contact for the first time.[1] This was a monumental shift that meant different things to different people depending on what adoption itself had meant. For some, adoption was the tragic and traumatic decision they had felt coerced into by familial or religious pressure. In some cases, it was not right to even call it a decision: newborns were forcibly removed from mothers who were unwed, or Indigenous—or both— sometimes minutes after they had given birth, and raised by more "suitable" families. But for other people adoption had simply been the blessing that allowed them to live as they wanted to by raising or relinquishing a child. As a follow-up review of the new legislation pointed out, these groups felt differently about the unsealing of the records: "For the former [group], it seemed indefensible for the law to continue to protect the secrecy of former times; for the latter, to open the records seemed grossly unfair, a retrospective law that betrayed the assurances of confidentiality which they saw themselves as having been given when they adopted children, or surrendered a child for adoption."

Some adoptive parents, like Peter's, had not yet told their child the truth, and some birth parents had gone on to have families who did not know that they had ever relinquished a child, so the law stipulated that both adoptive parents and birth parents could lodge a "contact veto." But, beset by health problems, Peter's mother had missed this memo. The women had knocked on her door, too, around the same time that they went to visit Peter, so the first she knew of the changes in the law was when she opened her door to Peter's biological mother and half sister. They visited several times, hoping to hear about Peter's life, before Peter found out. During those conversations, Peter guesses, his mother must have mentioned that he lived just a few streets over.

"I think she was in a state of terror and unable to deal with that," Peter says. "Once that happened, it was never going to end well, was it? Why she didn't just say, 'Oh, well, the game's up!'? I don't know, but I think she was just terrified of being abandoned." Instead, she phoned her sister in a panic to ask what was going on, and her sister wrote to the Department of Social Services to find out. Weeks passed. "Her sister was applying pressure, saying, 'You have to tell him, you have to tell him.'" But before she could, the department's reply went straight into the pile of mail that lay on the hall table for Peter to pick up.

"So she says, 'Did you ever think you might have been adopted?' It's funny—you never have the reactions to things that you think you'll have. Immediately, I could see that this was the moment [my mother] was thinking that I would walk out the door and she'd never see me again."

But it wasn't. Peter wasn't angry; he wasn't even upset.

"It was a sense of gratitude, you know, 'I wasn't even your child, and you gave me all of that?' I was feeling very special that I'd been so lucky to have ended up with those parents. I said to her, 'You weren't a perfect mother, but you were as close as it gets.'"

After that conversation, Peter kissed his mother good-bye, went home, and cried in the garden for two hours.

"The sobbing, I never understood. I think I was upset because my father was dead by then, and I never got the chance to reassure him...I was very close to my father, and when he died it was catastrophic for me. I remember one of the things I was thinking about in those floods of tears was: 'He must have always had this thought that if I found out I'd reject them.' There was a great sense of lost opportunity—I could have reassured him that I had the most wonderful father of all time."

In fact, after that day, his only real question was how he'd managed to get so far in life without finding out.

"My mother couldn't understand it. [She said] later, 'We kind of assumed that someone at school would say something and that would be the trigger, but that didn't happen, and then suddenly you're going through puberty, so that seemed like the wrong time, and then you're on the train going off to university...' So they just stopped thinking about it. I think there was a kind of instinct like: *Why rock the boat now?*"

By the facts of the case this looks like the textbook rational change of mind. Peter believed something, namely, "the woman who raised me is my biological mother." He then received overwhelming evidence against that belief, and discarded it. So it might be surprising to hear that this isn't a story about how Peter changed his mind. Instead, it's a story about how he didn't: how his attitudes and emotions toward his family made a Houdini-like escape from the river they'd just been thrown in and pulled themselves to shore, soggy but broadly unchanged.

"It's very difficult for people to understand—it invariably comes up at dinner, and you think, 'There goes the dinner party.' I told the story just the other night, and everyone automatically assumed that I would be outraged that I had been lied to by my adoptive parents, and they were the baddies. In fact, I had to sort of say, 'Look, I can't honestly say I would have wanted it any other way.'"

The revelation that you are not biologically related to the people you call family could affect rather more of us than we'd like to admit. Politely termed a "nonpaternity event" in genealogical and legal circles, the effect amplifies over generations, so by the time you're claiming a bloodline connected to someone ten generations ago, your chances of actually being biologically related are only slightly better than turning up tails in a coin toss. Even claiming bloodlines of two or three generations is perilous nowadays, as the boom in online DNA testing exhumes long-buried family secrets and forces radical mind changes about who is whose real father and what anyone really knows about the people they live with anyway.

For many people who have to change their minds in this crowbarred way, the thought of retaining their previous relationship and closeness just isn't an option. Sometimes when we change our minds about the people we love, we change our minds about whether we love them at all.

San Francisco residents Danny and Andrea Ramirez thought they were full siblings until a test from a DNA analysis company revealed they did not share both parents. California local Jaclyn Baxter discovered her dad had fathered three half siblings whom she had never met. Then there's the particularly unfortunate biologist who found himself in his own Greek tragedy when he sent his DNA for testing, hoping for a fun example to use in his class on genomes, only to discover he had a half brother who was born squarely during his parents' marriage. He agonized over whether to say anything to his father, and ultimately did; the information caused his parents' divorce. "We're not anywhere close to being healed yet and I don't know how long it will take to put the pieces back together," he wrote in a pseudonymous article for *Vox*.[2]

What is the rational response here? Do changes in the facts rationally necessitate changes in feeling? Peter's discovery seems not to have made a dent in the way he felt toward his family. Should it have?

Some people might think it's peculiar of me to even use the vocabulary of "rationality" to ask why Peter didn't change his mind about how much he loved his family. There's no way to change your *mind* about love, they might say. After all, love is an emotion, and emotion and reason would never speak if they met at a party.

I may as well come clean and tell you that I hate this stupid argument, because the widespread thought that reasons have nothing to do with emotion lets us get away with two fairly egregious pieces of bullshit.

The first is that it lets us think that emotions, just by virtue of being emotions, are irrational. If they are not reacting to facts and reason, then they cannot be reacting to facts and reason *well*, and voilà! Any time your argumentative opponent is emotional, they (actually it's often "she" who hears this complaint) are therefore being irrational.

The second piece of bullshit this argument lets us get away with is thinking it would be futile to try to change our minds, or other people's, about how they feel—because if emotions are not reacting to facts and reason, then they cannot be reacting to facts and reason *badly*. Too many times to count, and with costs I don't care to count, I've seen people simply give up on trying to change an emotional person's mind, citing as justification the fact that the person was emotional, when what was most needed was for someone to stay the persuasive course. I owe this view to a previous professor of mine, Sam Shpall, who has worked extensively on love and rationality, both as independent topics and insofar as they relate to each other. Shpall once taught a seminar on love, where half the class was dating the other half, and he was totally oblivious to the havoc he was wreaking on their relationships each week by assigning us readings that exposed more and more intrarelationship disagreement about what love means and what it demands. In an interview on ABC Radio National's *The Philosopher's Zone*, Shpall noted that one of the consequences of the widespread view that love is blind is that our reasonable friends, who are usually more than happy to try talking us out of bad friendships and bad jobs, will almost never try to talk us out of damaging romantic love.[3]

Besides, plenty of other emotions seem capable of being rationally grounded in fact. I once tweeted an offer of a $100 reward for someone, anyone, to come and kill one of those flying cockroaches with the whirring armored wings that had taken up residence on the baseboard in my bedroom. My thudding heart and sweating palms would have testified that I was extremely emotional. I was filled with fear. Does this mean that I was immune to persuasion or that facts and reasons had no purchase on how I felt? Of course not; if I had found good evidence that the shape I thought was a cockroach was in fact something else—like, for instance (to speak purely hypothetically, with no resemblance to actual events or persons, living or dead), a discarded date I had forgotten to sweep up—I would no longer be afraid. Fact, meet feeling: the intense emotional nature of some mental states does not prove that it is uninterested in reason or matters of fact.

It makes sense, then, to ask why the discovery of certain facts *wouldn't* make us change our feelings. Niko Kolodny, who is among other things a father, a professor at the University of California at Berkeley, and a philosopher of reason and emotion, puts the point thus: "Emotions are nonvoluntary responses, but at least some emotions are responses to reasons."[4]

But is love one such emotion? Not all emotions are; as Kolodny later wrote in an *Encyclopaedia of Philosophy* entry about love, which one hopes never to have to look up, "It is unclear what fact about one's beloved might warrant one's love for this person." If only some emotions, like anger, or fear, are open to persuasion by fact, perhaps my question about Peter is bunk after all: his love didn't change when the facts did for the simple reason that facts don't change *love*, and the question about whether that was rational therefore does not arise.

After all, if my love for you is based on the things I believe about you—which, based on your choice of reading material, I take to be things like your unassailable cleverness and wittiness—then am I not compelled to stop loving you if those things turn out to not be true? This is less funny when we apply it to actual marriages or long-standing friendships. If I fell in love with a partner for his brains and sense of adventure, it seems grotesque to conclude that rationality demands my feeling of love must change when those facts did—when he began to suffer from dementia and preferred to stay indoors. As everyone's favorite romantic, William Shakespeare, put it in everyone's second-favorite sonnet, "Love is not love / Which alters when it alteration finds."[5]

And if I love people for the facts that are true about them, am I not then compelled to love anyone for whom those things are true? Or worse, am I compelled to trade in the person I love for someone who has *more* of those love-justifying features? This seems an icky conclusion. "The lover who is constantly asking whether her beloved is the funniest, the prettiest, or physically the strongest of the persons in her acquaintance, seems not to be a genuine lover at all," wrote Troy Jollimore, a poet and professional philosopher whose work on love is laced with case studies taken from the great romances of literature.[6] His chapter on the ways love makes us "beyond comparison" opens with a letter that the young Russian poet Marina Tsvetayeva wrote to Rilke as he was dying: "You are not the poet I love most," she wrote. "'Most' already implies comparison."

And those are just the problems we run into when we say love is based on facts about character; what about if we say that love is based on facts about identity, as we seem to say about familial love? Just for fun, in writing this, I asked people why they loved their mothers or their children or their brothers and so on. Almost nobody replied with a character appraisal, which is just as well—if character appraisals grounded familial love, nobody would make it out of their adolescence still loved by the parents who knew them going in. If you're a parent, don't relax yet; plenty of children love their parents in spite of rather than because of the facts about their character. As novelist Zadie Smith said during an interview on NPR's *Fresh Air*, one of the strange features of the parent-child relationship is the way children can destroy their parents' self-image by seeing straight through to the hypocrisies and self-deception underneath.[7] A child's love for a parent often transcends, rather than responds to, an evaluation of character.

Instead, when I asked people why they loved their families, people answered with a simple fact, like "She's my mother." But quite quickly we arrive back at the problem Jollimore was worried about vis-à-vis the transferability of reasons for love: Did the discovery that the woman at the door was Peter's mother give him rational reason to love her?

Often, when we say things are "rational," or based on reasons, we mean there is a right and wrong way to respond to those reasons. As an old debating teammate of mine once said, impersonating the sorts of hyperrationalists we were surrounded by, "You think I *like* holding my beliefs? I am *compelled*, by the power of logic!" How are we meant to parse cases like Peter's, where it seems like there is a reason for feeling love, but it's entirely up to us whether to take it?

"One of the most shocking after-effects you can have from that moment," says Peter, "is meeting your birth mother...

It's like, for me, [as if] I was walking down the street with you, and you just pulled a woman out of the crowd and said, 'This is your mother.' [I'd] just stare at her and think, *Don't be ridiculous*. [I'd] just look into her eyes and see nothing. That's what I could never get over: that moment of 'This isn't real.'"

Peter made an effort to make a relationship with his birth family. It was a relief for both of them to have found each other. She knew he had thrived and been well taken care of; he knew she was no longer in turmoil about where he was. He met the rest of his biological family, and he got to know his half sister who had come to the door. He heard from his birth mother about his father. He started doing research on their family tree and was surprised to find how emotional he was when he found he had relatives who had been killed in the Bosnian War. But after the initial flurry of finding each other, he never quite got past the feeling that they were acquaintances who had been pulled together by circumstance.

"The birth-family thing was a fantasy I tried to play along with for a while, but…what was real for me was my adoptive family. The way I talk, my physical mannerisms, my sense of humor come from my [adoptive] parents. You know, I see shows on TV where people are being reunited after fifty years, and they're rushing across the tarmac to each other's arms… I always think they must have felt something was missing, and this is the 'restoration' moment, whereas for me there was no need of restoration."

The strange thing in all this is that if Peter *had* changed his mind—if he had felt that being lied to for so long was a problem for his relationship with the people who'd raised him, or if he had rushed across the metaphorical tarmac—it would be difficult to tell him he was wrong. Both reactions were available to him, and both were reactions to facts: What is the love that compels us to race toward a perfect stranger if not a reaction to a fact about that stranger? But it seems hard to find a rational rule to govern the space of available reactions.

"After Mum died I went into this sort of mode like, *Oh my god, there's probably all these members of the family thinking, 'Do we tell him? Don't we tell him?'*, so I gathered them all together and said, 'Look, I know. You can relax.' I remember my father's sister came to stay with me, and we went for a walk along the beach one day, and I said, 'Aunt Mary, I have to clear something up. I have this terror that you're in turmoil about whether to tell me that I'm adopted or not, but I know.' And she said, 'I'm so relieved. I think about it every day.'"

He even started to laugh about it.

"I spoke to some people I went to school with about it. I said, 'Did you know that I was adopted?' and they said, 'Peter, *everybody* knew you were adopted.' I said, 'Why didn't anybody ever *say* anything?!' They just said, 'You didn't ask.'"

Sometimes we feel helpless when we have to change our minds about the facts about the people closest to us. It can feel like there's no choice but to lose the feelings, too. Thousands of people will find themselves in Peter's literal position, tens of thousands more will discover family secrets, and thousands more will face questions about whether they do or should love the person opposite them. We know too well the confusion of these moments when nothing feels further away than the idea of reason.

In many ways, Peter deserves the credit for an ideally rational change of mind under these circumstances. He did not block out the evidence, deny it, or bend himself in cognitive loops telling fictional, comforting stories. He did not collapse in shame or internal disarray. He just accepted the truth.

But in many other ways, his response illuminates the sheer number of unanswered questions about what rationality consists of and what it asks of us, questions we each bang up against whether we know it or not as we try to change our own and other people's minds. Do we do best by focusing on rationality, or is it like happiness—if you aim right at it, you'll miss it? What makes our emotional responses "apt"? Which facts should matter to us, and how should we decide? Are these questions that rationality is silent on, or have we just not been listening?

Toward the end of our conversation Peter said, laughing, "This feels like therapy." In truth I'd felt that way in a lot of the interviews I'd done for this book. They had been stories of such massive upheavals, moments where the bedrock and everything on top of it started to shake. "A revelation like that could destroy you," as Peter put it. "I think I was lucky. My sense of self must have been fairly strong." It had felt intimate to hear stories of these moments, to hear the ways people pressed forward out of chaos without answers to the questions about what to believe and why.

I was struck by how varied their paths to truth had been, but how uniformly they looked back on their mind change as something to be proud of instead of as a moment of shame or defeat. I was struck by how often muddy, ordinary things— like whom they trusted or what they valued—had helped them find the truth and live through its consequences. It had felt personal to hear all these things, like being invited into the secret belfry of someone's mind to peer around at all the ropes.

And it made me all the more bitterly disappointed to keep turning on the TV and finding a climate of public argumentation that treats changing minds as combat—or, worse, entertainment—by trading on the lucrative fiction that being reasonable is just being really good at arguing. It's a comforting idea, surrounded as we are by so much endemic unreasonableness. But as an account of rationality, it is both philosophically impoverished and utterly inapplicable to the fragile intimate moments when we need it most. I look at our public debates now and see an abdication of our intellectual duty to the nuances of rationality and, more important, an abdication of our duties to each other.

How I Learned to Stop Worrying

I do not know the answers to many of the questions I've asked in this book. Instead, I think each story, just like one of Peter's model sets, is a miniature of a much larger complex sprawl: a reminder that rationality itself may turn out be as tangled, as knotty, and as rooted in reality as the minds it hopes to change.

A Postscript About People Who Strap Themselves to Rockets

So how do I change someone's mind? That's the question I keep getting, when I tell people I've been thinking about rational persuasion.

It's not hard to see why the question feels especially urgent at the moment. Intractable, evidence-resistant, and flat-out bigoted views seem to have a monkey grip on current consciousness. Brexit happened; Donald Trump was elected; a man strapped himself to a homemade rocket to prove the earth was (is) flat. Fully 77 percent of Americans believe that mainstream news outlets deliberately report "false or misleading news"; in 2016 *This American Life* reporter Zoe Chace had the following exchange with a Republican member of the South Dakota House of Representatives:[i]

ZOE CHACE: From my perspective, as a national reporter, there's still the Constitution. There's no Sharia anywhere.

AL NOVSTRUP: You don't think there's Sharia anywheres in the United States?

ZOE CHACE: Correct.

AL NOVSTRUP: I think you need to read more.

ZOE CHACE: I do read.

AL NOVSTRUP: You don't think there's Sharia any place in the United States? You don't think—wow. OK. You don't think there's Sharia? I'm just blown away. We're living on two different planets.

What is there to say that is unobvious? We've heard it all. We know that in the right alignment of circumstances, the results curdle marrow, like when Robert Gregory Bowers walked into a synagogue in Pittsburgh and—allegedly—opened fire, moments after he had posted on social media, "I can't sit by and watch my people get slaughtered," or when Edgar Maddison Welch took an assault rifle to Comet Ping Pong Pizzeria in Washington, DC, where he shot the walls and ceiling of the restaurant because he believed—along with others on Reddit and 4chan—that hacked emails from DNC chairman John Podesta revealed that the restaurant was the secret headquarters of a Democratic Party–led pedophile ring.

I have never liked the label "post-truth era," or the way it permits us to be nostalgic for a "truth era," a mythical time when partisan splits didn't predict the way people would consume their news, when the sensational didn't move faster copy than the actual, or when people didn't prioritize sources that confirm what they already believed. I think in some ways it's better to call this the "bullshit era," drawing on Harry Frankfurt's famous distinction between a liar and a bullshitter: a liar has to care about the truth in order to conceal it; the bullshitter just doesn't care. Whatever label we put on the mood around us, it's hard to disagree that things feel especially grim. It's hard not to hope that books with titles like *Stop Being Reasonable: How We Really Change Our Minds* will give us some sort of antidote.

Here is the bad news: I cannot, with any confidence, give you a guide to changing a given person's mind. I cannot present a set of strategies that will take one of the problems in this book, like "I'm not being given enough credibility" or "My loved one is ensnared by loyalty to an in-group that says outsiders can't be trusted," and map it to a solution that will make the people around you reasonable. The ways we deviate from rationality—and find our way back to it—are too idiosyncratic and too rooted in luck to admit of this kind of generalization. Anyone who says they have a persuasive strategy that will change a person's mind without first knowing their circumstances or the genealogy of their beliefs is either lying or grievously mistaken.

The good news is that we may each be able to find our own answers. The questions I have asked throughout these stories are about how we should think about changing minds, rationally speaking—about what sorts of strategies we might overlook by declaring them "irrational" or outside the sovereignty of reasoned debate. My hope is that the stories in this book help illuminate some of those strategies, help us see that we may have overlooked them in our pursuit of our ideal of reason, and invite each of us to do our own work joining the dots to our own lives.

I often see lessons about mind changing like the ones I got from these stories. Missy, Dylan, and their dissent-punishing sect made me see something about how hoodwinking authority figures claim their credibility at the expense of others', and thereby seek to silence our ability to reason for ourselves. Alex and his stint on *Faking It* showed us something about the hall of mirrors we can get trapped in when we try to reason logically about ourselves and the (rational) case for deciding to make self-truths instead of waiting to discover them. Nicole's dilemma about her own memory showed me something about uncertainty: the way it is nearly intolerable to stay uncertain about something in our sense of self, but easier to bear if we can make that belief less load bearing. Peter and his discovery about his mother taught me something about which facts emotions can react to, a comfort to those of us who have had to wonder, like he did, whether we can love a person who has deceived us. Even Zac and Mike in our postcatcall conversation in that alleyway showed me something about testimony, and the way we acquire knowledge—or fail to—just by speaking to each other.

Each of these stories took a natural supposition about reason and tested it against a real person's change of mind. The result, at least for me, is a case for a more capacious account of what it is to "be reasonable." Without proper attention to the actual human processes that make up these moments of changing minds (or failing to), we might not have thought that emotion or the ways we relate to each other, or our sense of self, have anything to do with "good" changes of mind.

What strategies do these revelations give us for those dinner-table exchanges that make us want to beat our interlocutors (and ourselves) about the head with the salt shaker?

If we hoped for answers under a silver cloche, what we got was philosophy's favorite bait and switch: more questions. But I would sooner have those questions, and the challenge of mapping them to the contours of our own lives, than the salve of answers from the old playbook of televisable debates. These questions give us new ways to look at the old problems. They help us understand where the wheels have been falling off. In many ways, they are the questions that really matter: What do I mean when I say "be reasonable"? Which paths might my friends and family have taken to their beliefs? When it comes to persuasion, where are the limits?

One limit we might discover is where we decide to employ the strategy of reasoned dialogue at all. I said at the outset that one reason for telling these stories is that if our public ideal of "rational persuasion" turns out to be wrong, we had better stop constructing our discourse around it, and fast. Each of the stories in this book gives us reason to think that, indeed, some of our practices rest on bad assumptions about rationality—the natural principles like "doubt everything" and "don't believe what you're told" turn out not to hold much water, and the idea that what we need is more "rational discourse" is not much use if it turns out that the philosophers I quoted in Chapter 1 are right and speech itself is vulnerable to the very power imbalances that it was supposed to help solve.

I want to close with some additional reasons to be suspicious of a few popular silicon-molded strategies for our current persuasive crisis, like "be empathetic" or "hear more from those we disagree with." There may well be individual moments where these strategies have their place—some of them are in this book. What alarms me is the apparent desire for these sorts of moves to be the *only* solution. Granted, it would be nicer if the apparent death rattle of rational discourse could be solved with simple changes in how we speak to each other. But the beliefs around us that most urgently require changing are profoundly complex in their origin and content, and the crisis the world faces is not just one of rationality but one of political and educational failure. I don't mean to sound grim, but I do mean the world; Brexit and Trump are just the anglophone instantiations of phenomena on the rise in Hungary, Brazil, and Venezuela, to say nothing of the places that have always been "like that." In many of these places, the relevant challenge is not just beliefs that need revising but a phenomenon that the work of philosopher Jason Stanley convinced me we should call by its proper name: propaganda. Stanley is the son of Holocaust survivors, and his companion pieces *How Propaganda Works* and *How Fascism Works* pull a frankly astonishing number of case studies together into an alarming analysis of the kindling and kerosene: it seems hard to ignore the fact that crises like the ones in these countries arise under conditions of monstrous inequality.[2] It seems hard to ignore that they share a sort of social Darwinism, a hierarchy of loyalty. It is difficult, with such an analysis in hand, to see a "bullshit era" as one that will be solved by having more of the same "both sides arguing on TV" that we have always had. In Stanley's words, "The problem of maintaining a stable liberal democracy, which requires free speech, given the problem of propaganda, does not have an easy solution (and anyone who thinks it does doesn't understand the problem)."

That's what I think, anyway. Here are some reasons you might want to join me.

First, employing "listening to each other more" as a strategy for changing minds writ large allows us to be blind to the actual content of what is being disagreed about. But the substance of a disagreement has massive implications for the strategies we ought to use in displacing it. For instance,

there are cases where empathy is pragmatically and rationally advisable: in cases like Susie's, for instance, where what
we need most is for someone to stay in touch with the truth
and not retreat from it out of shame. But there are cases
where empathy has neither rational nor pragmatic grounds,
like—on Kate Manne's analysis—misogyny or white supremacy, where a driving force behind a set of beliefs is the subterranean sense of being "owed" something. "Listening and
offering sympathy to those who are prone to shame-based
misogynistic as well as racist outbursts is feeding the very
need and sense of entitlement that drives them in the first
place, when they go unmet. In other words, it's adding fuel to
the fire, at least in the long term."[3]

Second, there are serious ethical questions about who deserves a debate. While it's tempting in the face of a racist relative to think that the solution is more critical dialogue, the
problem is that the very act of seeking to persuade someone
involves recognizing them as reachable, or as a member of the
moral community (albeit sometimes a member-in-waiting).
There are live questions about whether these people deserve
that esteem. Sometimes the position that someone espouses
is one that opposes the very underpinnings of the idea of mutual dialogue.

Third, we can only debate what our opponents explicitly
avow. Certain sorts of belief trail clouds of cultural imagination often not explicitly known to the person we are arguing
with; they do not know why they see being "uncaring" as a

particularly egregious vice from a woman or why the thought of migrants committing acts of sexual violence against white women grips them so violently. It is extraordinarily difficult to drag these coded associations to the surface; as Charles Mills wrote in his seminal *Black Rights/White Wrongs*, "The white delusion of racial superiority insulates itself against refutation."[4] In part the problem is one of interdependency: "Perception, conception, memory, testimony, and motivational group interest...are all constantly in interaction with one another. When the individual [is] perceiving, he is doing so with eyes and ears that have been socialized....A separation of elements [will] necessarily be artificial, and each element so extracted bears a ghostly trail of all the others in its wake." Even if we could disentangle one from the other long enough to argue with it, that's not all it's worth arguing against: the ultimate aim should be to bring the entire system into the argumentative crosshairs. Tough ask, for one "reasonable debate."

Finally, when we have "rational discourse" with people, we tend to regard them as sincerely invested in their position. Indeed, this was a central part of why Supreme Court justice Louis Brandeis thought free speech mattered. "[The founding fathers] believed that freedom to think as you will and to *speak as you think* are means indispensable to the discovery and spread of political truth," he wrote.[5] But lately it looks as though both sides aren't speaking as they think, or at any rate that the things one side might see as evidence are not themselves sincere. Macedonian teens make thousands of dollars by posting fake news on Twitter; Trump alters his slogans midspeech, sniffing out applause like a truffle pig; even claims to sincerity are themselves branded. When Al Franken published his book *Lies and the Lying Liars Who Tell Them: A Fair and Balanced Look at the Right*, Fox News sued him: "fair and balanced" was their trademark.[6]

This is not an argument against speaking to each other. It is an argument against speaking to each other in the ways we always have, with the same presumptions about which debates work and why.

I know it would be far more satisfying to hear that all we need to do is find ways to connect emotionally with our opponents or learn to stop being so blinded by "partisan hate." And indeed there may be good reasons for each of those strategies, in certain particular circumstances. But as a uniform approach to the problem of intractably unchangeable minds, I am suspicious of the way they exempt us from having to pay attention to the lineage and complexity of the problem. In this way, these proposals remind me of the spate of early-2017 speculation by a host of psychologists and commentators that Donald Trump had narcissistic personality disorder. I thought the whole thing smelled of a fevered hope that the president's actions and, more puzzlingly, his appeal would need no further explanation than a prepackaged, easy-to-understand deviation from the neurological norm: he's sick—

that's it. Psychologist Allen Frances, who quite literally helped write the criteria for narcissistic personality disorder, eventually wrote to the *New York Times* in frustration: "Psychiatric name-calling is a misguided way of countering Mr. Trump's attack on democracy.... The antidote to a dystopic Trumpean dark age is political, not psychological."[7]

We want our problems of "unreachable opponents" to be comparably simple. It's easy to want to wash our hands of any deeper understanding of the sorts of conspiracies that populate our discourse by seeing them in logical terms: they're bad arguments, and good ones will help. It spares us having to confront the vast spiraling history of patriarchy, white supremacy, and disparities in wealth and education that led to these beliefs. It spares us having to ask what is true of money and power in the United States such that the people who have both tend to benefit from the spread of ignorance.

I know it's unsatisfying to not have the answer. But it *should* be satisfying. It should be exciting to look at the challenge of rational persuasion by wondering what we can glean from the real. There is a king's ransom of worthwhile material we can learn from, if we can accept that there is something *to* learn. My hope is that the stories in this book help us to look on these problems with fresh eyes and help us to wonder whether that inquiry might begin in the same place we want it to end up—with real stories, and the moments that change them.

Acknowledgments

I most wish to thank the people who have trusted me to tell their story: Dylan, Missy, Alex, Nicole, "Susie," and "Peter," who cannot be thanked by name. I hope to have captured even half of their strength, imagination, and optimism.

I am profoundly grateful to Colleen Lawrie and the team at PublicAffairs for the chance to undertake this project and their endless patience as I changed my mind about what exactly that project was.

I am also deeply indebted to Jeff Shreve and Peter Tallack at the Science Factory, who have been most encouraging and thoughtful literary agents and who have read and reread the work here for as long as I have been writing it.

My particular thanks to Emma Driver, who edited with insightful care and eye-watering speed. Emma, as always: almost a pleasure.

Acknowledgments

To these professors and mentors I owe a special debt: Caroline West, Kate Manne, and Susan Brison, whose work gives me the answers when I wonder "What's the point of philosophy?," and Tom Dougherty. Any philosophy of value I ever produce is due to him; anything bad is because I didn't listen properly.

Graduate students at Princeton, Sydney, and Pittsburgh Universities were valuable sounding boards and at times admirable foes, particularly Brett Karlan, who is both.

Adam Madigan bought me a lot of food once, saying, "Thank me if you ever write a book." Adam, thank you, and my heartfelt gratitude to Tess Lyon, Emmanuel Dzotsi, Dan Dixon, and Daniel Kenny. Without you life would be much poorer, and this book would have been finished much sooner.

Ned Howells-Whitaker cannot be thanked in ways that fit on the page. For showing me subtleties and beauty I had often missed in life and in philosophy, I am forever glad you changed my mind.

Finally, my parents, Michael and Claire, whose conversation at the dinner table made my grandmother worry for the girl who had to keep up with them, have spent decades being inspiring mentors and generous readers. Without their support, I could not have written this book, or done any of the things that came before it.

Notes

Introduction:
Everything Was Protein Powder and Nothing Hurt

1 This chapter title is in homage to Kurt Vonnegut's phrase "Everything was beautiful and nothing hurt" in his 1969 novel, *Slaughterhouse Five*.

2 The Center for Applied Rationality and the self-excusing remarks of many applicants were covered by Jennifer Kahn, who reported on the workshops by enlisting herself in one: Kahn, "The Happiness Code," *New York Times*, January 14, 2016, www.nytimes.com/2016/01/17/magazine/the-happiness -code.html.

3 Stanley Cavell on the willingness to forgo knowing: Cavell, *Disowning Knowledge in Seven Plays of Shakespeare* (New York: Cambridge University Press, 2003).

4 Jerry Fodor reviews John McDowell's *Mind and World*: Fodor, "Encounters with Trees," *London Review of Books*, April 20, 1995, www.lrb.co.uk/v17/n08/jerry-fodor/encounters-with-trees.

5 Antonin Scalia and Bryan A. Garner in *Making Your Case: The Art of Persuading Judges* (St. Paul, MN: Thomson/West, 2008).

chapter one:
A Treatise on the Ways Your Dick Is Not Like
This Burrito

1 *This American Life* radio piece: "Once More, with Feeling," *This American Life*, December 2, 2016, www.thisamericanlife .org/603/once-more-with-feeling.

2 Simone de Beauvoir on a woman's "objective resistance": de Beauvoir, *The Second Sex* (Paris: Gallimard, 1949).

3 John Milton on "Truth": Milton, *Areopagitica: A Speech of Mr. John Milton for the Liberty of Unlicenc'd Printing, to the Parlament of England* (1644).

4 The *New York Times* on its white nationalist article: Marc Lacey, "Readers Accuse Us of Normalizing a Nazi Sympathizer; We Respond," *New York Times*, November 26, 2017, www.nytimes.com/2017/11/26/reader-center/readers-accuse -us-of-normalizing-a-nazi-sympathizer-we-respond.html.

5 Response by the Festival of Dangerous Ideas organizers: Simon Longstaff, "Thinking the Unthinkable: Was Honour Killings Too Dangerous an Idea?" *ABC Religion & Ethics*, June 30, 2014, www.abc.net.au/religion/articles/2014/06/30/4035870 .htm.

6 Miranda Fricker on "testimonial injustice" and *To Kill a Mockingbird*: Fricker, *Epistemic Injustice: Power and the Ethics of Knowing* (Oxford: Oxford University Press, 2009).

7 José Medina's work on background credibility allocations: Medina, *The Epistemology of Resistance: Gender and Racial Oppression, Epistemic Injustice, and the Social Imagination* (New York: Oxford University Press, 2013).

8 Kate Manne's work on misogyny: Manne, *Down Girl: The Logic of Misogyny* (New York: Oxford University Press, 2017).

Notes to Chapter One

9 Rush Limbaugh's remark about "yanking the media's chain": Michael Inbar, "Rush Limbaugh: I Love to 'Yank Media's Chain," *Today*, October 13, 2009, www.today.com/news/rush-limbaugh -i-love-yank-medias-chain-1C9014016.

10 Rae Langton's work on silencing, in particular of sexual re- fusal: Langton, "Speech Acts and Unspeakable Acts," *Philos- ophy & Public Affairs* 22, no. 4 (1993): 293–330. Further work by Langton on similar topics: *Sexual Solipsism: Philosophical Essays on Pornography and Objectification* (New York: Oxford University Press, 2009).

11 Quotes in the paragraphs about Luke Lazarus and Saxon Mul- lins are from the retrial, the judgment of which is available in *R v. Lazarus* [2017] NSWCCA 279.

12 Ben Fordham's words to Luke Lazarus are quoted in "Exclusive: Ben Fordham Confronts Luke Lazarus," 2GB, May 17, 2018, www.2gb.com/exclusive-ben-fordham-confronts-luke-lazarus/.

13 Study on perceptions of women's speaking time: Anne Cutler and Donia R. Scott, "Speaker Sex and Perceived Apportionment of Talk," *Applied Psycholinguistics* 11, no. 3 (1990): 253–272.

14 Study on women and men showing "expertise": Maria Brann and Kimberly Leezer Himes, "Perceived Credibility of Male Versus Female Television Newscasters," *Communication Re- search Reports* 27, no. 3 (2010): 243–252.

15 Social experiment concerning effects of race on perception of bicycle handling: Stephen Williams, "WATCH: Racism Takes Center Stage as Actors One White, One Black—Pretend to Steal a Bike," *New York Daily News*, June 10, 2013, www.ny dailynews.com/news/national/watch-white-black-bike-thieves -treated-differently-article-1.1368401.

chapter two:
Faith; or, George Michael Was Wrong

1 G. E. M. Anscombe on testimony: Anscombe, "Hume and Julius Caesar," *Analysis* 34, no. 1 (1973): 1–7.
2 David Hume on testimony: Hume, "Of Miracles," in *An Enquiry Concerning Human Understanding* (1748).
3 C. A. J. Coady on testimony: Coady, *Testimony: A Philosophical Study* (Oxford: Clarendon Press, 1992).
4 Dan Ariely on people confiding in him: Ariely, *Predictably Irrational: The Hidden Forces That Shape Our Decisions* (London: HarperCollins, 2008).
5 Edward J. Craig's work on social epistemology: Craig, *Knowledge and the State of Nature: An Essay in Conceptual Synthesis* (Oxford: Oxford University Press, 1990).

chapter three:
Fake It 'til You Make It and/or Forget Who You Are

1 Alex's *Faking It* episode: "Alex the Animal," *Faking It*, Channel 4, UK, September 18, 2000.
2 Julian Baggini's remark about "essential me-ness" appears in the Peter Goldie work I mention at length: Goldie, *The Mess Inside: Narrative, Emotion, and the Mind* (Oxford: Oxford University Press, 2012).
3 Marya Schechtman on the narrative self: Schechtman, "The Narrative Self," in *The Oxford Handbook of the Self*, ed. Stephen Gallagher (New York: Oxford University Press, 2011), 394–418.
4 Roger Ebert in *Life Itself: A Memoir* (New York: Grand Central, 2011).
5 Stephen Grosz on the incoherent story: Grosz, *The Examined Life: How We Lose and Find Ourselves* (New York: W. W. Norton, 2013).

6 J. David Velleman's fabulous remark about rabbits and hats, which he does not use in the crude way that I have: Velleman, "The Self as Narrator," in *Autonomy and the Challenges to Liberalism: New Essays*, ed. John Christman and Joel Anderson (Cambridge: Cambridge University Press, 2005), 56–76.

7 Geoff Dyer, *Out of Sheer Rage: Wrestling with D. H. Lawrence* (New York: North Point Press, 1997).

8 Much of the thinking about "true" selves as analogous to art is owed to Alexander Nehamas on the intention of artists: Nehamas, "Nietzsche, Intention, Action," *European Journal of Philosophy* 26, no. 2 (2018): 685–701.

9 Laurie A. Paul on transformative experiences: Paul, *Transformative Experience* (Oxford: Oxford University Press, 2014).

10 Amia Srinivasan on "the selves we might become": Srinivasan, "All the Same," *Times Literary Supplement*, June 10, 2015, www.lapaul.org/papers/tls-review.pdf.

11 Peter Goldie on the unstable self: Goldie, *Mess Inside*.

12 The Harvard study: Liz Mineo, "Good Genes Are Nice, but Joy Is Better," *Harvard Gazette*, April 11, 2017, https://news.harvard.edu/gazette/story/2017/04/over-nearly-80-years-harvard-study-has-been-showing-how-to-live-a-healthy-and-happy-life/.

chapter four:
The Hard Drive and the Camel's Back

1 Clarence Darrow on doubt: Darrow, *The Story of My Life* (New York: C. Scribner's Sons, 1932); Christopher Hitchens on surrendering skepticism: Hitchens, "Holier than Thou," *Penn & Teller: Bullshit!*, Showtime, May 23, 2005, www.dailymotion.com/video/x4rqa6s.

2 Oliver Crowell's remark: Crowell, letter to the general assembly of the Church of Scotland, August 3, 1650, www.oliver cromwell.org/Letters_and_speeches/letters/Letter_129.pdf.

3 Joseph Ratzinger and sexual abuse in the Catholic Church: Jamie Doward, "Pope 'Obstructed' Sex Abuse Inquiry," *Guardian*, April 24, 2005, www.theguardian.com/world/2005/apr/24/children.childprotection.

4 René Descartes on doubting all things: Descartes, *Meditations on First Philosophy* (1641); on forfeiting four years of work: letter to Marin Mersenne, April 1634.

5 William K. Clifford's treatise on belief: Clifford, "The Ethics of Belief (1877).

6 Deborah Schurman-Kauflin's article in *Psychology Today*: Schurman-Kauflin, "What Predators' Wives Really Know," *Psychology Today*, April 21, 2012, www.psychologytoday.com/blog/disturbed/201204/what-predators-wives-really-know.

7 Seth Meyers's article: Meyers, "The Wives of Pedophiles Often Know the Truth," *Psychology Today*, June 23, 2012, www.psychologytoday.com/gb/blog/insight-is-2020/201206/the-wives-pedophiles-often-know-the-truth.

8 The *New York Times* reader on Sue Klebold's memoir: "Careerista," quoted in Lela Moore, "Readers Respond: 'A Mother's Reckoning,'" *New York Times*, February 18, 2016, www.nytimes.com/2016/02/18/books/review/readers-respond-a-mothers-reckoning.html.

9 Dottie Sandusky's son on what his mother knew: Matt Sandusky quoted in Sean Carlin, "Sandusky's Son Speaks Out on Abusive Childhood," AP News, December 5, 2014, https://apnews.com/dfbe49f27d7940d4a490b4394c33763d.

10 Matt Lauer's interview with Dottie Sandusky: *Today*, March 12, 2014, www.today.com/video/today/54648895; Alexander

Abad-Santos, "The Depth of Dottie Sandusky's Denial Is Alarming," *Atlantic*, March 12, 2014, www.theatlantic.com /national/archive/2014/03/depth-dottie-sanduskys-denial -alarming/359091/.

11 William James's description of "snarling logicality": James, "The Will to Believe," address to the Philosophical Clubs of Yale and Brown Universities, 1896, www.gutenberg.org /files/26659/26659-h/26659-h.htm.

12 An example of Annette Baier's work on betrayal of trust: Baier, "Trust and Antitrust," *Ethics* 96 (1986): 231–260.

13 D. O. Thomas on the importance of trust: Thomas, "The Duty to Trust," *Proceedings of the Aristotelian Society* 79 (1979): 89–101.

14 Victoria McGeer on trust being "rational": McGeer, "Trust, Hope and Empowerment," *Australasian Journal of Philosophy* 86, no. 2 (2008): 237–254.

chapter five:
Learning to Forget What You Never Really Knew

1 David Corwin's interview transcripts: Corwin, "Transcripts from Interviews with Taus, Nicole, 1983–1996."

2 Clarence Darrow on agnosticism: Darrow, "Why I Am an Agnostic" (1929).

3 David Hume on evidence: Hume, "Of Miracles," in *An Enquiry Concerning Human Understanding* (1748); William K. Clifford's principle: Clifford, "The Ethics of Belief" (1877).

4 Blaise Pascal's wager: Pascal, *Pascal's Pensées* (1669–1670).

5 David L. Corwin's published report into Nicole's case: Corwin and Erna Olafson, "Videotaped Discovery of a Reportedly Un-recallable Memory of Child Sexual Abuse: Comparison with a

Childhood Interview Videotaped 11 Years Before," *Child Maltreatment* 2, no. 2 (1997): 91–112.

6 Elizabeth F. Loftus and Melvin J. Guyer's two-part article on Nicole's case: Loftus and Guyer, "Who Abused Jane Doe? The Hazards of the Single Case History," pts. 1–2, *Skeptical Inquirer* 26, no. 3 (2002): 24–32, www.csicop.org/si/show/who_abused _jane_doe_the_hazards_of_the_single_case_history_part_1; no. 4 (2002): 37–40, www.csicop.org/si/show/who_abused_jane _doe_the_hazards_of_the_single_case_history_part_2.

7 William James on chasing truth and avoiding error: James, "The Will to Believe," address to the Philosophical Clubs of Yale and Brown Universities, 1896, www.gutenberg.org/files/266 59/26659-h/26659-h.htm.

8 Richard Feldman on the difference between epistemic options and practical ones: Feldman, "Clifford's Principle and James's Options," *Social Epistemology* 20, no. 1 (2006): 19–33.

9 Tyler Burge's work on justifications for and entitlement to beliefs: Burge, "Content Preservation," *Philosophical Review* 102, no. 4 (1993): 457–488.

chapter six:
How I Learned to Stop Worrying and Love the Truth Bomb

1 Follow-up review of the changes to New South Wales adoption law: NSW Law Reform Commission, *Review of the Adoption Information Act, 1990: Summary Report*, Report no. 69, 1992, www.lawreform.justice.nsw.gov.au/Documents/Publications /Reports/Report-69-outline.pdf.

2 The biologist who found he had a half sibling: George Doe [pseud.], "With Genetic Testing, I Gave My Parents the Gift of Divorce," *Vox*, September 9, 2014, www.vox.com/2014/9/9/5975

653/with-genetic-testing-i-gave-my-parents-the-gift-of-divorce
-23andme.

3   Sam Shpall on the strange preferential treatment of romantic
    love: ABC Radio National. "Love Has Its Reasons," *The Phi-
    losopher's Zone*, April 16, 2017, www.abc.net.au/radionational
    /programs/philosopherszone/love-has-its-reasons/8433712.

4   Niko Kolodny on love: Kolodny, "Love as Valuing a Relation-
    ship," *Philosophical Review* 112, no. 2 (2003): 135–189; "Love
    [addendum]," in vol. 1 of *Encyclopedia of Philosophy*, ed. Don-
    ald M. Borchert, 2nd ed. (Detroit: Macmillan Reference USA,
    2006).

5   Shakespeare's sonnet: Sonnet 116, "Let me not to the marriage
    of true minds..." (1609).

6   Troy Jollimore's view on love: Jollimore, *Love's Vision* (Prince-
    ton, NJ: Princeton University Press, 2011).

7   Zadie Smith on *Fresh Air*: "Novelist Zadie Smith on Historical
    Nostalgia and the Nature of Talent," *Fresh Air*, January 20, 2017,
    www.npr.org/2017/01/20/510600755/novelist-zadie-smith
    -on-historical-nostalgia-and-the-nature-of-talent?t=1542366
    299663.

Epilogue:
A Postscript About People Who Strap Themselves to Rockets

1   "600: Will I Know Anyone at This Party?," *This American Life*,
    December 14, 2017, www.thisamericanlife.org/600/transcript.

2   Jason Stanley, *How Fascism Works: The Politics of Us and Them*
    (New York: Random House, 2018); Stanley, *How Propaganda
    Works* (reprint, Princeton, NJ: Princeton University Press,
    2016); Stanley, "How Fascism Works: A Reply to Peter Ludlow,"

Notes to Epilogue

Politics/Letters Live, January 10, 2019, http://politicsslashlet
ters.live/features/how-fascism-works-a-reply-to-peter-ludlow/.

3 Kate Manne, *Exonerating Men* (Oxford University Press, 2017),
www.oxfordscholarship.com/view/10.1093/oso/9780190604981
.001.0001/oso-9780190604981-chapter-7.

4 Charles W. Mills, *Black Rights/White Wrongs: The Critique of
Racial Liberalism* (New York: Oxford University Press, 2017).

5 Quote from Brandeis: *Whitey v. California*, 274 U.S. 357 (1927)
(emphasis added).

6 The lawsuit against Al Franken appears in Sam Leith, "On
Post-Truth: How Facts Became Irrelevant in the Modern
World," *Times Literary Supplement*, August 16, 2017, www.the
-tls.co.uk/articles/public/post-truth-sam-leith/.

7 Allen Frances's letter to the *New York Times*: "Opinion: An
Eminent Psychiatrist Demurs on Trump's Mental State," *New
York Times*, December 22, 2017, www.nytimes.com/2017/02/14
/opinion/an-eminent-psychiatrist-demurs-on-trumps-mental
-state.html.

Index

Index

Austin, J. L., 47
author, having relationship with an, 131–132
authority as person, words and exercising one's, 47
authority figures, claiming credibility at expense of others, 75–78, 190

Badar, Urthman, 34
Baggini, Julian, 90
Baier, Annette, 132
Baxter, Jaclyn, 175
Beauvoir, Simone de, 31
"be empathetic," as strategy for persuasive crisis, 192, 194
behavior, being rational and, 8–9
being believed, in argument, 44–45
"being rational," behavior and, 8–9
"being reasonable," 17
  behavior and, 8–9
  evidence and, 9
  See also "be reasonable"
belief
  cost of withholding, 159–162
  credibility and accepting someone's word for, 74–76
  doubt and, 116–117
  entitlement to, 161
  ethics of, 9

evidence for, 59–62, 137, 145–146
indecisive evidence and withholding, 153–155, 161–162
loss of faith in people telling one what to believe, 69–73
that earth is flat, 187
three options for, 160
uprooting foundational, 14–15
in what one is told, 56–57, 59–60, 67
withholding, 145–148, 153–155, 161–162
See also religious sect
believing what we're told, 56–57, 59–60, 67
  ability to consider other sources and, 76–78, 80–81
  deference loops and, 82–83
"be reasonable," what it means to, 191. See also "being reasonable"
betrayal, trust and risk of, 132
Big Brother (television program), 86
Black Rights/White Wrongs (Mills), 195
Bowers, Robert Gregory, 188
Brandeis, Louis, 195
Brexit, 187, 192–193
Bridalplasty (television program), 86

212

Index

Index

Index

Index

Index

Index

Index

shame
  changing minds and
    avoiding, 14
  for not realizing truth about
    loved ones' immoral acts,
    127–128, 129–130
Shpall, Sam, 176–177
shunning, of wayward religious
  sect members, 55, 58, 77
The Simple Life (television
  program), 86
sincerity, doubting claims to,
  195–196
Skeptical Inquirer (journal),
  152
skepticism
  Hitchens on, 114
  personified, 130–132
  Sextus Empiricus and, 6
  as strategy for avoiding
    vulnerability, 132
  See also doubt
smiling, women and autopilot,
  30–31, 39
smiling as evidence
  that women are
    uncomfortable, 28–31
  that women like catcalling,
    25–26, 27–28, 31
Smith, Zadie, 180
Smurfs, 55
social Darwinism, 193
speech, power imbalances and,
  192

"Speech Acts and Unspeakable
  Acts" (Langton), 47–48
Srinivasan, Amia, 106
Stanley, Jason, 193
State of the Union (television
  program), 2
subconscious incubation,
  conversion moment and,
  72
subjugation, treating others as
  subject as tool of, 81
Susie (wife of sex addict and
  child molester)
  learning about husband
    John's secret life, 112–113,
    118–121
  learning husband John was
    child molester, 122–125
  response to trusting wrong
    person, 133–135
  shame for not realizing truth
    about husband, 127
  trust in husband, 125

testimonial injustice, 35–36
testimony
  acquiring knowledge via, 62,
    191
  as evidence, 62
  reliance on, 53, 62
This American Life (radio
  program), 3–5, 20, 23–24,
  40, 42, 43, 187
Thomas, D. O., 132–133

Index

White Ribbon Campaign, 45
white supremacy, 194, 195, 197
"Who Abused Jane Doe?"
    (Loftus & Guyer), 152–153,
    156–157
Wittgenstein, Ludwig, 11–12, 61
"The Wives of Pedophiles Often
    Know the Truth" (Meyers),
    126
Wollstonecraft, Mary, 19
Woolf, Virginia, 85
words
  argument and disappearing,
    36–37, 42

argument and warping of,
    37–38, 43
do not work the same way for
    everyone, 34–35, 43, 46–48
The World (Descartes), 116

Zac (catcaller), 190–191
belief women like being
    catcalled, 25–28
interviewing without friend
    Mike, 40–42, 43
refusal to consider women
    do not like being catcalled,
    28–30, 32, 38–39, 40–42

CREDIT: NED HOWELLS WHITAKER

Eleanor Gordon-Smith is a philosopher, radio producer, and recovering debater working at the intersection of academic ethics and the chaos of ordinary life. Currently at Princeton University, she has contributed to *This American Life*, the CBC, the Australian, the *Sydney Morning Herald, Meanjin,* and *The Philosopher's Zone.*

PublicAffairs is a publishing house founded in 1997. It is a tribute to the standards, values, and flair of three persons who have served as mentors to countless reporters, writers, editors, and book people of all kinds, including me.

I. F. STONE, proprietor of *I. F. Stone's Weekly*, combined a commitment to the First Amendment with entrepreneurial zeal and reporting skill and became one of the great independent journalists in American history. At the age of eighty, Izzy published *The Trial of Socrates*, which was a national bestseller. He wrote the book after he taught himself ancient Greek.

BENJAMIN C. BRADLEE was for nearly thirty years the charismatic editorial leader of *The Washington Post*. It was Ben who gave the *Post* the range and courage to pursue such historic issues as Watergate. He supported his reporters with a tenacity that made them fearless and it is no accident that so many became authors of influential, best-selling books.

ROBERT L. BERNSTEIN, the chief executive of Random House for more than a quarter century, guided one of the nation's premier publishing houses. Bob was personally responsible for many books of political dissent and argument that challenged tyranny around the globe. He is also the founder and longtime chair of Human Rights Watch, one of the most respected human rights organizations in the world.

· · ·

For fifty years, the banner of Public Affairs Press was carried by its owner Morris B. Schnapper, who published Gandhi, Nasser, Toynbee, Truman, and about 1,500 other authors. In 1983, Schnapper was described by *The Washington Post* as "a redoubtable gadfly." His legacy will endure in the books to come.

Peter Osnos, *Founder*